Intangible Cultural Heritage of South India

Intangible Cultural Heritage of South India

Editors

Sarit K. Chaudhuri

V. Jayarajan

GYAN

Indira Gandhi Rashtriya Manav Sangrahalaya
(National Museum of Mankind Bhopal)

First Published, 2020

Published by
Gyan Publishing House
5, Ansari Road
Daryaganj, New Delhi-110002
Phone: 9811692060
E-mail: books@gyanbooks.com

and

Indira Gandhi Rashtriya Manav Sangrahalaya
Shamla Hills, Bhopal
Phones: 0755-2661290, 2661319
Fax: 91-755-2661458

Printed at: G. Print Process, Delhi.

Cataloging in Publication Data--DK
Courtesy: D.K. Agencies (P) Ltd. <docinfo@dkagencies.com>

Intangible cultural heritage of South India / editors, Sarit K. Chaudhuri, V. Jayarajan.
pages cm
"... national seminar conducted by IGRMS in association with Folkland, International Centre for Folklore and Culture and Kannur University, Department of Malayalam during Taittireeyam 2015 ..."--Intoduction.
ISBN 9788121214834

1. India, South--Civilization--Congresses. 2. India, South--Social life and customs--Congresses. I. Chaudhuri, S. K. (Sarit Kumar), editor. II. Jayarajan, V., editor. III. Indirā Gāndhī Rāshṭrīya Mānava Saṅgrahālaya, organizer, publisher.

LCC DS484.4.I58 2019 | DDC 954.8 23

Contents

Acknowledgement

This volume is made possible because of the sustained support of Prof. Saritkumar Chowdhury, Diretor of IGRMS, who had proposed the idea of conducting a National Seminar in connection with the celebration of Taittireeyam to mark the 25th anniversary of Folkland and publishing the papers presented in the seminar. I wish to thank him for his continuous support and encouragement from selecting the scholars to a seminar to convert those manuscripts into a memorable piece of tangible cultural heritage. Prof. Chaudhary has also favoured me through his scholarly forward, which adds to spice up the specimen.

I wish to thank Prof. A.M. Sreedharan, Director, and P.K. Rajan Memorial campus of Kannur University for conducting the seminar at his Neeleshwaram Centre.

Mr. Sudhir Srivastava need to be appreciated for compiling the seminar literature with his editorial acumen.

I have received the invaluable guidance with utmost care, diligence and affection from Mr.T G Sajeev, of IGRMS for the success of Taittareeyam festival. I acknowledge the efforts of Dr. Sankar Rao and Rashmi Shukla of IGRMS for accomplishing this seminar in connection with Taittareeyam festival.

My family members need to be recalled on the occasion from wife Smt. Sarinjini Jayarajan, daughters Athira and Arathi for their invaluable suggestions and guidance from time to time.

The volume is dedicated to my beloved mother Smt. V. Thankam, who bereaved us quite recently. Also my mentor Kavalam Narayana Panikkar, who remained as the light house in the assimilation of state's cultural ethos- folk to classical theatre; rustic to classical music, folk to classical dance.

My dedication is only a meagre effort towards the renaissance of intangible cultural heritage.

V. Jayarajan

List of Contributors

1. **Dr. Sadanand B. Sugandhi:** Assistant Professor, P. G. Department of Anthropology, Karnatak University, Dharwad, Karnataka.
2. **Dr. V. Pragati:** Associate Professor, Department of Anthropology, Puducherry Institute of Linguistics and Culture Puducherry, Email: pragathirajkumar@yahoo.co.in.
3. **Dr. B. Vijendra:** Anthropologist Anthroplogical Survey of India, Mysore.
4. **Dr. Nilanjan Khatua:** Anthropological Survey of India, Southern Regional Centre, Mysore Email-nilanjan_k1@yahoo.co.in
5. **Rajesh Patniak:** Exploration and Research Group, Visakhapatnam. Hous No-07, MIG-40,Sai Avenue, Pithapuram colony maddilapalem, Visakhapatnam, Andhra Pradesh 530003
6. **B. V. Raviprasad:** Anthropological Survey of India, Southern Regional Office, Mysore.
7. **Jesurathnam Devarapalli:** Assistant Professor, Department of Anthropology, Pondicherry University, Puducherry – 605014, E.mail: drjesudev@gmail.com
8. **Sreejisha V.P.:** Research Scholar, Department of Anthropology, Pondicherry University, Puducherry – 605014, E-mail: sriju07@gmail.com
9. **Dr. H.K. Bhat:** Retd. Professor of Anthropology, University of Mysore and General Secretary, Society for Indian Medical Anthropology (SIMA), 771, 5th Cross, Roopanagar, Mysore, Karnataka 570026 E-mail: hkbhatmysore@gmail.com

10. Dr. S.B. Konale: Vice President SIMA, 771, 5th cross Roopapa Nagar Mysore, Karnataka,570026, 11 Varun Thampan, PhD Scholar Department of Anthropology Kannur University, Palayad, Thalasseri, Kannur, Kerala

12. Dr.V.Jayarajan: Chairman Folkland Elamnbachi Kasargod, Kerala 671311 folkland@rediffmail.com

13. Prof. P. Subbachary: Head, Department of Folklore and Tribal Studies Dean, School of Human and Social Sciences Dravidian University,Kuppam, Andrapradesh

14. Shobha Shivaprasad Nayak: School of Classical Kannada Studies, Rani Channamma University, Belagavi, Karnataka, India. Email: shobhan535@gmail.com

15. SINI.M, Assistant Professor, Department of Anthropology, Kannur University, Thalassery Campus, Palayad 670661.

16. Jayawant B. Ambekar: Former Professor of Sociology, Shivaji University, Kolhapur:416004.

17. Dr. D. Satyanarayana: Anthropological Survey of India Central Regional Centre CGO Complex, 1st Floor Seminari Hills Nagpur 440006

18. Shruthi T.V.: Research Scholar, Kannur Unuiversity, Dept of Anthropology,Palayad, Thalasseri, shruthigdas@gmail.com

19. G. Suryanarayana: Sr. Photo Journalist & Rtd. Sr. Manager (Vizag Steel) Plot No.18, Balaji Nagar, Desapatrunipalem Visakhapatnam-531021.A.P. Email:suryagarnepudi@gmail.com

20. Dr. K. M. Raghava Nambiar: Panchamoola, Journalists' Colony Near Indrani Temple P.O. Kunjibettu, Udupi 576102

Introduction

Traditions and intangible cultural heritage puts together seventeen research papers, which were presented in the national seminar conducted by IGRMS in association with Folkland, International centre for folklore and culture and Kannur University, Department of Malayalam during Taittireeyam 2015, a festival to mark the 25th anniversary of Folkland. All the papers except three were presented in the seminar conducted on 11 and 12th of May 2015 at Kannur University, P.K. Rajan Memorial Campus, Nileswaram in Kerala.

The papers reflect the vivid facets of sociocultural practices, customs and festivals, worships and practices prevailed across Indian states. This volume inter alia deals with ethnographic studies, observations as the outcome of intensive field works, essays on performative context, gender and ecological issues examined through scientific analysis using multiple parameters.

Dr. K.M. Raghava Nambiar in his paper titled 'Some observations on traditional theatres of South India', mentions some southern traditional theatres and the striking feature that invariably they have with puppetry. He points out the strong evidence to prove that Indian theatre as a whole is highly indebted to string puppetry. The term 'Sutradhara' of Sanskrit drama indicates of to have originated from string puppetry. Sutradhara means string holder. Similarly, when looked at Kathakali performance of Kerala from a distance, it looks like an activity of moving dolls. The way of movement of face, hands etc., reminds of a puppet. Perhaps, Kathakali is the theatre form that retains maximum signs of puppetry in it. Almost all Indian dances began as the imitation of puppetry, which was regarded once upon a time as the main means of worship. This status of puppetry still exists in East Asian countries. He talks about the rice belt culture and how the traditional theatres had been attached to agriculture in coastal Karnataka and Kerala. There is enough scope for thinking that the people belonging to different occupations the follow traditional theatre as a cult. This independent theatre cult might have served them fulfil their educational, religious and cultural aspirations. The religious aspect of theatre has boosted their morale in carrying out day-to-day work and to succeed in life.

Smt. Shobha Shivaprasad Nayak from the School of Classical Kannada Studies, Rani Channamma University, Karnataka, in her paper 'Quilt' as the Folk-Art: A Study' discusses about its importance and the need to save this heritage. The contemporary collage and Batik arts were being inspired by the age old quilt art. There is no age bar for making quilt. Some do it as hobbies, some for livelihoods and some choose as a profession. Belgaum northern Karnataka leaving 'Mannettina Amavase' (special festival on moonless night) the rest of the days they make quilt on. There is a community called as 'Gondaligas' who makes quilts and sell. Old/wore out and colourful pieces of cloth are the major requirement for making quilt. The old generation people use *kudogolu* to cut the clothes. The small needles are being used to design and the main stitches are being done by big needles. She has also discussed the quilt making methods, types, designs and specialities. With the progress in technology and life style, the quilts gradually started disappearing from the lives of workers. Quilt weavers have been deprived of any means of government support, neither in the form of finance, promotion nor support. Hence, if the government input initiates necessary in identifying this rich art and provide them financial and technical support, the rural art could grow towards the height of popularity and cultural heritage.

Dr. V. Jayarajan in his paper 'Mudiyettu', ritual dance drama tradition of Kerala' describes the mythology behind Mudiyettu and the rituals for its performance. After scrutinizing the merits thoroughly, Mudiyettu was inscribed in the Representative List of Intangible Cultural Heritage of Humanity by UNESCO in 2010 as per decision of the 5.COM 6.17. After the inscription in the representative list of ICH of humanity, Mudiyettu became more popular amongst the national and international audience. Moreover, the inscription could raise awareness about the significance of Intangible Cultural Heritage by offering an example of social harmony among different castes and communities.

In their joint paper, Keddasa: a ritual associated with land and cultivation in Tulunad coastal region of Karnataka, the authors Dr. H.K.Bhat and Dr. S.B. Konale, talk about Keddasa, a land cultivation ritual of Tulunad observed on 27th, 28th, 29th and 30th days of the tenth month of the Tulu calendar. By Keddasa, the people believe of Tulunad the Tulu mother or the mother Earth is becoming bride Keddasa observation is based on the belief that the Mother Earth suffers from the pangs of menstruation which is a symbol of fertility. The women observe by cleaning a little space in the front yard and offering the requirements of a purificatory bath: Hunting and meat eating is associated with its observance by non-vegetarian food consumers. According to them, the origin or the originators of rituals and the socioeconomic conditions prevailing at its origin is not known. It is also very difficult to exactly pinpoint the objectives behind starting of such ritual. On interviewing people of different strata, men, women, young and old belonging to different castes in the two villages and outside Tulunad, they believe on in the motherhood of the Earth and the femininity of mother Earth. Though they do not believe in the anthropomorphism of Earth in its physical form, they do not also believe in the anthropomorphism in certain states and values of the Earth. It is this belief which has made them believe in the menstrual cycle of the Earth. They are not worried about the scientific proof. Some Brahmana scholars on adopting those customs say that they believe in Rigvedic injunvtion of adopting noble thought from every corner of the universe and some say it as Manu's injunction to adopt local customs, when one migrates into other places, unless such practices do not affect their basic value system. Rituals of Keddasa in general symbolizes, the world view, the religious beliefs and the human values and the social relations among the Tulu people with respect to Mother Earth.

Dr.V. Pragati, Associate Professor, PILC, Pudhucherry in her paper, Socio-Religious Aspects among *Arundhathiyars* of Puducherry' presents socio-religious aspect of Puducherry *Arundhathiyar* in village settings. The religious life of *Arundhathiyars* was analysed with the help of three methodological terms, viz., sacred centers, sacred specialists and sacred performances, if conceived together, they may be termed as "sacred-complex". The sacred centers of the *Arundhathiyars* are being located at a number of places, viz., in the house, courtyard, cattleshed, within the settlement, village outskirts, and in the neighbouring places. The deities enshrined are being represented by stones or rocks of different colours, trees, spears, iron rods and trident. Practically, no significant change is found perceptible in the religious and ritualistic behaviour of *Arundhathiyars*. The impact of technological and materialistic modern culture has not been as powerful as that of religious culture on them. Worships and other religious acts are part and parcel of their daily life. However, the so-called modern and sophisticated youngsters seldom conform to these ideals, though the old and the aged still live up to them. Lastly, it is concluded that the *Arundhathiyars*, like most other castes of Puducherry attach prime importance to religious practices in every lifestyle. Human life as perceived by them is replete with hazards that makes them seek the help of supernatural beings. *Arundthathiyar* presents a colorful panorama of religious faiths and practices, which is the manifestation of rapport with their cultural-ecological conditions. It conceives man as passing through a life surrounded by the *peey-picacu* (evil-spirits) and *kaatu-karupu* (wind-spirits) company of powers and elements, mostly impersonal in character. Some of these are being regarded as presiding forces' over various faculties of life, each having the sphere of influence. These are diligently propitiated to ward–off dangers associated with their influence.

Dr. Nilanjan Khatua's paper entitled 'Contributions of Dr. Mathur to the Study of Fisher folk' highlights on the contribution of an anthropologist in the field of ethnographic study of fishing community and their world. It is Dr. P.R.G. Mathur who was the responsible official of Anthropological Survey of India busy in extensive research, particularly in the field of Anthropology of marine fisher folk in India. Dr. Nilanjan quotes Dr. Mathur to have given considerable space to factors of fishing technology and rituals. The study does not convey any clues whether the household census carried out during the field work as found from some of the Census statistics. He did not discuss about the political institutions and any political interference among the fisher folk in her study. Dr. Mathur has used various local terms which throws light on the intensive fieldwork he had of association with the native Mappila fisher folk. He not only collected the empirical data from the fisher folks of Kerala, but also tried to give the scientific input with the consultation of marine biologists on the environment and oceanography.

'Kinship and Religion in the context of a Nayar Lineage: A Study' by Varun Thampan, Ph.D Scholar, Department of Anthropology, Kannur University talks about the religious life of Nayar lineage. He points out that it showed right from the inception; characteristic features that are unmistakably in little tradition as well as the very tradition. The conduct of *Theyyam* belongs to little tradition, whereas ceremonies that employ Brahman priests fall with the great tradition. One concept of universalisation and parochialisation can also be seen in this case. *Paraliamma* is parochialised form of Mookambika Devi, universalisation is in action by linking *Kuttichchatan* to Lord Vishnu. The members of this lineage in contrast with their aboriginees have become more involved in the great traditions of Hinduism. They visit Hindu holy centres like Guruvayur, Sabarimala, Kollur and Palani. Many have become better versed in the philosophical aspects of great Hindu traditions like Epics and Puranas. In spite of that faith in traditional religious practices from temporary eclipse - have remained intact. Despite total destruction of lineage as a corporate entity with political, economic and military role and as a property owning body, matrilineage remained intact as the unit of kinship even to this day. One survival of matrilineal kinship ensured that religious notion built into that kinship has also survived. It was only because of this reason that a revival of traditional sacred practice was feasible.

A paper titled "Intangible cultural heritage and Sustainable economic development: A case of pot makers of Kannur District, Kerala by Ms. Sini M, an Assistant Professor of the Anthropology Department of Kannur University discusses about the tradition of pot making in the district. She has identified different challenges faced by them like –lack of quality raw materials, outdated production, lack of skill upgradation and capacity building, lack of value addition to products, lack of adequate market linkages are being a few. This paper suggests them maintain and achieve sustained development of traditional economic sectors, especially craft to safeguard the cultural heritage. Investment and support in this locale is very essential to withstand the future situations for sustainable, consistent, proficient resource mobilisation.

Dr Jayawant B.Ambedkar, a former professor of Sociology at Shivaji University, Kolhapur talks about the conflict and the effects of developmental projects on the Dange Dhanagars of Radhanagri taluk, Kolhapur district, southern Maharashtra through his paper titled "Indigenous communities and their role in conserving ecological and cultural heritage: A case study of Dange Dhanagars". He highlights on the importance of sustainable cultural and economic practices of smaler communities who live on in the nature cradle. As approach is based on the intermittent fieldwork during 1992-00. Though, it is declared by the United Nations that there was no conflict between the development and environment. The Dange Dhanagars case study we ought to have an appropriate combination of the above approaches.

"Intangible Cultural Heritage of Tribes in Eastern Ghats of Andhra Pradesh: A Methodological Approach for Cultural and Visual Documentation"- a joint paper by Rajesh Patnaik and B V Raviprasad describes the methodology of Visual and Descriptive Documentation of "Intangible Cultural Heritage" of those tribes living in the north eastern ghats of Visakhapatnam district, Andhra Pradesh. The objectives of the study includes identifying the systems of folk knowledge, collection of myths, tales, rituals, celebrations and festivals, understanding of the traditional craftsmanship, mapping of cultural variation on spatial basis, correlating them in traditional knowledge to biodiversity, identifying cognitively considered traditional cultural aspects on the verge of disappearance.

Mr.G.Suryanarayana's paper, titled "Intangible cultural heritage of South India" tries to highlight "The Intangible

Cultural Heritage" being observed by the devotees at the famous Simhachalam temple in Andhra Pradesh. The temple is situated on Simhagiri Hills, 18 Kms away from Visakhapatnam city on the eastern ghats at a height of about 250 mtrs above the sea level. The presiding deity is Varaha Lakshmi Narasimha combining the iconographic features of Varaha and Narasimha. The devotees from remote and rural areas, mostly in groups along with mentors, visit the temple and perform appropriate rituals before entering the sanctum-sanctorum. This paper throws light on the interesting and unique rituals being performed at this temple.

In their paper, "Development Induced Displacement and Adaptive Impediments of Aranadan of Malappuram", Jesurathnam Devarapalli and Sreejisha V P investigate on the end results of the Development Induced Displacement (DID) among the Aranadan tribal group of Malappuram district, Kerala. The plantation construction and population redistribution schemes introduced by the government led to developmental issues in the area and this paper expressed the opinion that DID is a 'socio-economic issue' associated with the interruption factor of the survival strategy of any indigenous community. The main finding of this study is that displacement of Aranadan, (who are hunters and gatherers to have sustained with the natural resources from the interior areas of Western Ghats) from their habitat due to deforestation and developmental schemes of government has resulted in their rolocating to new habitat, mostly colonised having 5 guntas of land for each household. The risks associated with those people, who wandered in the dense forest subsisting on hunting and gathering was that they had been through a stage of cultural shock as well as skill demand. The displacement along with have lead them lose their access to resources. The authors recommend Aranadan the that required employment skills for them, especially during rainy season.

Dr. D. Satyanarayana in his study on "Bathukamma – the most popular intangible heritage of Telangana" describes Bathukamma detail in a festival of flowers celebrated as the most popularly festival of Telangana. It forms an intangible heritage of Telangana since preserved only by oral / folk traditions until 18th century, when Kanchanapalli Narasimharaju, a native of Mogilicherla of Warangal district, had written about the mystic origins and the beauty of floral deity Bathukamma. The author has made attempts to study the historical evolution of the deity since Bathukamma is folk deity, which is not so easy to trace her origins. It is also noted that the people of Telangana used Bathukamma as a symbol of unity and united means of strength during the struggle for separate state of Telangana between 2001 and 2013. This is the reason why the new government of Telangana has made the Bathukamma as the official festival of the state, to be celebrated with groandeur.

Dr. B.R.Vijayendra's paper "Health status among the Yeravas of Karnataka" discusses a genre of medical anthropology. The Yerava is a Scheduled Tribe of Karnataka, mainly settled in the Virajpet taluk of Madikeri district in Karnataka. The concept of health varies from one culture to another, the term 'health' for the Yerava is a state of having a good conditioned body. Health is an important aspect in the life of the Yerava. The author also reminds that the attribution of some illnesses to certain deities, spirits, sorcery, fear and evil eye is due to the fact that the Yeravas have not changed in their traditional modes of beliefs and practices related to health and illness.

Dr. Niranjan Khatua, in his paper on "Contributions of Dr. Mathur to the Study of Fisherfolk" highlights on the contribution of Dr. P.R.G. Mathur, a renowned anthropologist in the field of ethnographic study of a fishing community and their world of fishing. "The Mappila Fisherfolk of Kerala" is his consequential publication

(1978), which claims as a landmark in the field of Anthropology. Mappila – Muslim fisher folks of Kerala, mainly inhabit in the Malabar coast of Kerala and is the universe of Dr. Mathur's study. They are expert fishermen with expertise in detecting the fish shoal under the changing conditions of the Arabian Sea. The author as that Dr. Mathur is a tireless fieldworker and matchless anthropologist, so believes far his contribution in the study and expertise of tribes and castes of Kerala is concerned. The author acknowledges his efforts in carrying out the study. Dr. Mathur his widely travelled in Kerala in various capacities and has written a good number of research papers and individual books. The author feels that Dr. Mathur's study of Mappila fisherfolks of Kerala, is a unique source of inspiration for the young researcher. He observes that him to have used various local terms, which throws light on the intensive fieldwork he has conducted and his association with the native Mappila fisherfolk.

"Women in folklore: A study of Makkappothi Theyyam in northern Malabar" is an analysis of myth in the context of women in folklore" – a paper by Shruthi TV analyses the myth of the *Theyyam Kadangode Makkam*, in an Anthropological perspective. It shows how the intangible cultural heritage of folklore and the norms symbolised in its performative manifestations are indicative of changing social norms on women's status, which are evoked in the myth of *Kadangode Makkam.* The Myth related to mother goddesses indicates that the woman who challenge the customs and traditions of patriarchy will be victimised, and are evolved as goddesses. The author believes the study of life and status of women and the importance of folklore had to be understood when we account for the life of ordinary women. The author believes that deities are creations of mind and their existence depends on faith. Women used this spiritual act as a strategy against the oppression and violence by the patriarchy. Those things which cannot be done in physical world are satisfied by attaining sacred power. Thinking and feeling of women's collective is revealed through this and their ideas are free from external influence. A Woman her faith in her own self, wisdom, and truthfulness she resigns herself to the fate despite. This can be taken as a form of resistance against the social system in which women are oppressed as they could not come out to show their resistance in the past, expressed it so through folklore.

Prof. P Subbachary's paper "A proding Telugu proverb and the embedded cultural history" delineates how a proverb hiding history of this society and alive still in the daily usage of Telugu society brings the cultural history into daily life. In this paper, Subbachary narrates three events where he was present and to have heard the proverb during performance. He has also heard this proverb in many other contexts in his village, right from his school days. He analyses them in three different contexts.

V. Jayarajan

1

Health status of Yeravas

— *Dr. B.R. Vijayendra*

General Introduction

Medical Anthropology has a broad mandate to understand and interpret humans, their diseases and illnesses, and their medical system. According to Merrill Singer and Hans Baer "As a social science, medical anthropology addresses not only specific health issues but also seeks to build a broad, theoretically based understanding of what health is, how culture and health interact, the role of social relations in shaping disease, and a range of other issues. In other words, medical anthropology seeks to understand health related issues and to use this knowledge in improving human health and well-being." (2007:9)

Medical anthropology makes use of a number of theoretical perspectives and the applied tradition focuses mainly on studying illness, beliefs with the aim of contributing to health interventions. Merrill Singer and Hans Baer's answer for the question why medical anthropology is that "because medical anthropologists, employing anthropology's traditional immersion methods for studying human life up close and in context, as well as the discipline's holistic picture of the human situation, a traditional disciplinary concern with understanding things from the insider's point of view and flow of experience, and an applied orientations to human problems, can make an important difference in the world" (2007:8). There has also been much discussion of the various meanings of disease, illness, and sickness (Brown et al. 1994; Hahn 1984, 1995; Kleinman 1980; Sedgwick 1981).

Introduction to the tribe and area

The Yerava is a scheduled tribe of Karnataka, mainly settled in the Virajpet taluk of Madikeri district in Karnataka. This tribal population unevenly distributed all over the state and the districtwise consideration discloses about a few pockets of higher concentration and that Madikeri is one such district. In the total district population of Madikeri, 8.23 percent belonged to Zcheduled tribes and Virajpet taluk happens to be an area of higher concentration.

Madikeri is a land of great antiquity. It drives name from 'Kodimalenad', which means a dense forest land on steep hills. It is the smallest district in the state with an area of 4,102 square kilometers. It lies in the southwestern border of the state between northern latitude 11° 56^{1} and 12° 52^{1} and Eastern longitude 75° 22^{1} and 76° 12^{1}. It is bounded by Hassan district on the north, by Mysore district on the east, by Dakshin Kannad district on the west and by Cannanore district of Kerala state on the south. The district is organised into three taluks viz. Madikeri, Virajpet and Somavarpet. Of these, Virajpet is the largest in area and Somvarpet is the smallest. There are in all 296 census villages. Forests and plantations are the twin pillars, which have for long been supporting the economy of the district.

Luiz found three main divisions: the Panjiri, Pani and Badavar or Badaga. 'Yerava' was a generic suffix; he listed them as different tribes. He had mentioned that Adiyan were known as Eravas (Yeravas) in certain facts. The name connotes them to be alienable with the land and were given to begging. Luiz made no reference to Kaji Yerava. The Pani Yeravas and the Panjiri Yeravas were enumerated during the 1871 and 1881 Census, separately. At the remaining Census, the Yeravas were considered as a single tribe.

However, the field study reveals that, the two important Yerava groups viz., Pani Yerava and Panjiri Yerava are actually two different groups and each form a part and parcel of a larger community spread over the border areas. The Badaga Yeravas is found around Kutta in the southeastern parts of Virajpet taluk, and traced their habitat to places in Heggadadevana Kote taluk of Mysore district. The Kage or Kaji Yerava also known as Kake Paniya is found in Habbale, Devarakadu and other villages in central Madikeri. They have been identified themselves with Pani Yerava and have lost distinctive characteristics if any.

The available sources indicate that Yeravas came from other area. 'Yerava' appears to be a name given to those groups by the Kodavas. The immigrant labour force was totally dependent on the land-owning people. The word 'era' in the Kodava language means 'to beg', and the ' erava' means 'beggar'. In Kannada, the words mean respectively, 'to borrow' and 'borrower'. These terms are applicable to these people, for, they had no resources; it was customary for the landlords to advance money and make them bonded labourers.

Yeravas are found in most villages of Virajpet and some villages in Madikeri and Somwarpet taluks in Madikeri district. They also live in a few villages of Heggadadevana Kote, Periyapatna and Hunsur taluks of the Mysore district. The Census 1981, projects their population as 19, 261. The Pani Yerava was the most numerous followed by the Panjiri. The other two groups account for only a few hundreds. The Yerava's settlements are called *Kunju*. Men wear cotton dhoti around the waist and waistcloth or knickers or '*cheddy*' as the undergarment. The young men are now more accustomed to the use of trousers than the *lungies*.

The women wear the saree covering the entire body from neck down to the ankles almost with the blouse almost covering the back. The manner of wearing saree by Yerava women resembles the traditional Kodava style. Women are fond of ornaments, which includes ear studs, nose-screw, bangles, *kailumudra* for toes, *mudra* for fingers, etc., which are made out of cheap metal.

The location of the present study

The present study was conducted in an interior Yerava settlement called Ayirhosalli situated inside of the forest about three kilometers from the other Yerava settlement Majjigalla. The settlement is situated 31 Kms from the taluk headquarter Virajpet and habituated by 41 Yerava families. The total population is 172 (89 males and 83 females) persons in those settlements, when 32 families cultivate forest land and other families were dependents on forest products and daily wages.

The settlement is situated inside the forest. There is no road between the settlement and bus stop. Only private buses ply on this route. The settlement is situated 3 kms from the bus stop. The village is situated by forest on three sides with agricultural land on the other side. All the 41 families having thatched huts and it is surrounded by split bamboo fencing. There is sufficient space for growing kitchen garden with a small space provided in the backyard for bathing. A stream flows aside the settlement and one out of two hand pumps is the source of water. The settlement is not electrified and a hospital is situated about 9 kms.

Personal hygiene and sanitation

The huts of Yerava are nucleus, usually built on a slope

by leveling out the house site. Appreciable open space around the hut helps in getting sufficient fresh air and light. They live in mud-walled, thatched huts built on a raised platform. The dwelling of Yerava consists of an open verandah with a raised platform in the front portion and a kitchen-cum-living room. The hut is usually kept clean. Once in a week the platform, courtyard and floor are smeared with a mixture of cowdung and charcoal powder. The huts have hardly any arrangements for light and air. As there is no proper exit for smoke, excessive smoke finds accumulated inside the hut. Due to poor ventilation, they won't get fresh air during nights. Usually, the woman takes bath in the backyard, where a small space is provided for the purpose: As huts are built on a slope there is no chance for stagnation of water. Clothes are being washed once in a week in the stream but during the summer, they wash either near the hand pump or in the backyard of the house. Due to this water accumulates near the hand pump, which favours the breeding of germs of different bacterial diseases. For defecation, they are accustomed to the habit of going in open field, but dogs and pigs do not allow the night soil to remain in the fields. In the backyard, temporary shed is being built for their domestic animals such as pigs and cows, which produces in sanitary environment through animal sources such as urine, feacas, saliva, etc. Stream and hand pumps constitute their main source of drinking water, but neither they filter nor boil it.

Table 1.1 Personnel cleanliness of Individuals (Bathing)

Sl. No	*Frequency*	*Male*	*Per cent*	*Female*	*Per cent*	*Total*	*Per cent*
1.	Daily	7	4.07	8	4.65	15	8.72
2.	Once in 3 to 4 days	33	19.19	38	22.09	71	41.28
3.	Once in a week	34	19.77	25	14.53	59	34.30

Regarding bathing practice, the frequency of taking bath is mainly dependent on climatic conditions; because of the cold climate they rarely take bath. It also varies from one age group to the other. The percentage is being calculated for the total population of 172. The data on bathing practice reveals that majority of person's i.e., 41.28 percent (19.19 percent males and 22.09 percent females) bathe once in three to four days, three to four days, preferably younger generation. About 34.30 percent persons (19.77 percent males and 14.53 percent females) bathe once in a week; most of them were middle-aged group. Children especially below three years of age bathe daily i.e., only 8.72 percent (4.07 percent male and 4.65 percent female). About 15.70 percent persons bathe on Mondays, especially those aged persons. 'They use soap as a cleaning agent, but prefer soft stone pebbles to scrub the accumulated sweat and dirt from the body.

Concepts of health and illness

Medical anthropologists have devoted considerable energy to examining conceptions of health and illness cross-culturally. While "health" and "illness" are everyday terms, what do they actually mean? The World Health Organisation (WHO) defines health as "not merely the absence of disease and infirmity but complete physical, mental and social wellbeing" (2007:63-64). The concept of health varies from one culture to another, the term 'health' for the Yerava is a state of 'full fitness', i.e., a healthy person has a good conditioned body and can carry his routine with full zeal. He can work hard and eat well. People believe that a healthy person can be identified through his face. The face is regarded as the index of health. Health is an important aspect in the life of the Yerava. Whenever two persons meet with each other, they enquire about one's health status i.e., "*Makkmari chandarnayilaro*"? It means "are the children doing well"? This shows them giving more prominence for children's health than others have least to withstand the effect of strong illness. The answer for the above question will be either positive i.e. "*parkaad chandamallaru*" which means 'not bad, all are keeping well' or negative one, i.e., "*kullariku suka kane*" which means 'somebody is not feeling well".

The terms '*chanda*' and '*suka*' mean 'health', but the wider meaning of the term is happiness. If a person has no *sukha*, it means he has some worries. The worries, worries relate to health, treated as the most complicated, because, it disturbs the overall activities of the family with sudden financial crisis.

The Yerava believe that lean and medium stature persons are healthier than short and tall. People believe that food is the main media for acquiring strength. They know that food consumed is going to convert into blood and as the quantity of food consumption reduces, weakness develops in the body. Meat, egg and milk are considered as giving food. Food is believed to be one of the prime factors for the good condition of health.

People believe the body of each individual is formed either of two elements, *ushna* (hot) and *sheetha* (cold). Based on the predominant element in the body, they classify the human body into *ushna mayee* and *sheetha mayee* inherited from birth. *Ushna mayee* (hot body) persons are believed to be lean and strong with higher working capacity and won't feel tired. Such persons usually suffer from inflammation with dry and chaffed skin, whereas *sthe heetha mayee* (cold body) category persons are believed to be less strong. The latter have comparatively less working capacity, and get tired soon and begin to sweat profusely.

The cultural interpretive in medical anthropology posits a distinction between disease and illness. The former constitute a natural entity that can be identified through various bodily signs, such as a high temperature, elevated blood pressure or rapid heart rate and (possibly but not always) a sense of physical and emotional discomfort on the part of a person (Kleinman 1980). The presence of a disease, in other words, is established through a diagnosis by a professional healer, like a physician of biomedicine (2007: 65). According to Merrill Singer and Hans Baer "Illness, by contrast, as it is often used in medical anthropology, constitutes a cultural construction that can be identified only through interpretive activities or narratives. Illness is rooted in a culturally constituted explanatory model that seeks to clarify the source of distress and to outline a course of treatment to be pursued by both the healer and the patient" (2007:65). So the illness can be interpreted as patient's experience of sickness. For the Yerava clan, the illness is a state of 'unfitness'. That means improper functioning of the body and not in a position to carry out the routine work. *Katta* is the term used to designate the illness. Most of the illness is thought to be caused on account of sins and crimes done in their life. Aside, the wrath of deities, spirits and magic powers are also considered as illness causing factors. They still have faith in wearing spells, talisman, and fate invoking divine powers.

Illness classification

The understanding of health and illness vary from one culture to another considerably in terms of what they regard to be the agents of illness. George Peter Murdock (1980) have devised most comprehensive typologies of folk categories of disease or illness. Typologies are framed, based on various causative factors of illness and the illness among the Yerava can be classified into five categories on the basis of etiological factors viz., deity-oriented illness (*Daiva kattu),* spirit-oriented illness (*Payee kattu*), fear-oriented illness (*Bedarike kattu),* Sorcery-oriented illness (*Maatada Kattu*), *kanndrusti* (evil eye) and physical body-oriented illness (*Maiya Kattu).*

Daiva kattu: The Goddesses Durgi, Chamundi, Chowdi, Maramma are the protectors. Their settlement should be propitiated with *harabara* (sacrifice), at least once in a year. Failure to perform the ceremony believed to cause d*aiva kattu,* namely plague, cholera, measles, *maripunnu* or destruction of the settlement, vomiting, dysentery, blood stained dysentery etc. The supernatural being is the causative factor for the occurrence of *daiva kattu,* wherein the wrath of various deities cause many illnesses due to the non-fulfillment of vows for a longer period.

Payee kattu: Payee means spirit and illnesses such as prolonged dysentery and vomiting, dull face, looking at one direction, child dies after birth, loosing consciousness, eating of red-coloured rice, eating of mud, tightening of body, paralysis etc are attributed to this category. It is believed to be not responding to any treatment. Angry ancestral spirits *achche payee* (grandfather's spirit) and *vithave payee* (grandmother's spirit) are believed to cause the illnesses like prolonged vomiting or dysentery, weakness, paralysis etc., from the nonperformance of yearly ceremonies. Intrusion of spirits (*payeeyatu*) is believed to intrude into the body of a person if s[he] passes through the spirit dwelling place alone, especially during nights. Women are said to be common victims of the spirit intrusion, as they ease in the field during nights. There are three types of spirits, *yelavat payee, handipayee* and *nirmali.*

Bedarike kattu: Bedarike means fear is believed to cause illness among children. Fever, dysentery, dull face, not taking food or milk is some of the fear-oriented illnesses.

Maata kattu: Maata means sorcery is believed to be made secretly with the help of sorcerer. Illness such as losing appetite, tightening of legs and hands, swelling of body or face or stomach, stupid behaviour, not talking with anyone, having distress, stomach pain, weakness, giddiness are of these category illnesses. Sorcery is one of the important causes of illness, in which *odi*, *kaisa* and *mata* are the types of prevalent sorcery among them. In *odi*, sorcerer inserts thorns into the body of the victim due to which tightening of legs and hands, that stiffles stomach, bulges body or face swells, behaving foolishly and sitting simply at one place making the person face stomach pain, weakness, no appetite, giddness and no strength in legs and hands. *Maata* is another method, in which the sorcerer adopts black magic over the victim. The victim loses stamina, has had piercing pain in the body and enlargement of his stomach. It is believed to cause death, if it does not eliminate in time.

Kanndrutsi: Evil eye *is also one of the causative factor of illness.* Some persons believe to have evil eye powers and children, well-built persons, and grown-up girls are the common victims.

Maina kattu: Are body linked illnesses caused due to wrong diet, environmental conditions, polluted water and worm infestation. Illnesses like common cold, inflammation of stomach, tooth ache, gastric, mouth sore, eczema, scabies, cuts, sore belong to this category. The *Yeravas* prefer herbal medicine for relief.

Diagnosis of illness

Diagnosis is very important aspect for finding out the causative factor of illness. There are mainly four types of diagnostic procedures adopted among the Yerava, viz., divine powers (through deity), cowrie shashtra (cowrie shell method), yellow water method and signs and symptoms method.

Thammadi or *kanneladi* are the diviners who are consulted to diagnose the illness caused by supernatural beings. Tuesday, Friday, full moon day and new moon day are considered as very auspicious. The family folks with the victim visit the diviners with coconut, incense sticks, betel leaves, areca nut, banana and flower.

Thammadi or *kanneladi* enters into trance after chanting verse and tells the cause of the illness and fix a day for removing the effect of the cause.

Shashthrakarai (diagnostician through cowrie) takes cowries in his hand and praise god and throws the cowries, like dice on lattice. Usually, he keeps nine cowries; odd considers positive and even as negative answer.

Yellow water (*manjalnir)* is also one of the diagnosing procedures to find out the cause of the *soku* (spirit intrusion). They prepare turmeric water or take cow's urine in a plate and keep a cow dung ball, whenever the victim has symptoms of *soku*. A wick is placed over the cow dung cake. Afterwards a cup or small vessel is kept upside down. If the cup or vessel catches tightly, then it is believed upon it that either deity or spirit has caused the illness *soku*. The other method, turmeric water is prepared and live charcoal is waved three times and rinsed in it. If the yellow water turns into red then it indicates the vctim to have exposed to *soku*.

Signs and symptoms is a very important diagnostic method.The medicine men administering medicine after hearing and observing the associated signs and symptoms thereby prepare its preparation. Colour is one of the features used in the process of diagnosis. If eyes and face turn red, it is then believed to be the sign of illness *soku*. If the face turns pale yellow or white, it is one of the sign of the illness *kaisa*. The behaviour is also considered as one of the features during diagnosis. If a patient behaves like a fool, it is a sign of *beppodi*, a sorcery illness and sitting silently speaking to anybody will be termed, *mankodi*. A patient behaves like a fool, eating red rice, eating too much and rubbing his nose are the signs of such spirit intrusion.

Ethno-medical specialists

While indigenous or tribal society's exhibit a diversity of healing beliefs and practices as well as an array of different kinds of healers, these tend to be rather loosely organised. It reflects the idiosyncratic patterns resulting in part from the fact that healers commonly are secretive about their medical knowledge (2007:121). Among the Yeravas, there is a diversity of healing beliefs and practices under different kinds of healers.

The *Thammadi* among the Yerava is designated as a priest. Usually *Thammadi* usually involves in priestly work, get possessed by the deity. He sifts through the cause of illness and other problems. He finds appropriate remedies through divine intuition. They are not full time priests nor is their post hereditary. The *kanneladi* is a head priest among the Yeravas, the post is not hereditary, but prefer to teach either to their sons or sister's son. They are also not full-time practitioners. People consider *Kanneladi* as a specialist in curing illness caused by supernatural beings, sorcery activities, evil eye, etc. through divine powers. Every Tuesday, Friday, full moon day and new moon-day, deity enters into his body. The deity solves all sorts of illness and problems, offering special *pooia* and sacrificial offerings can possess him. The *kanneladi* is not supposed to smoke *beedi,* chew tobacco, drink arrack and have sexual intercourse on these days. The *Kanneladi* cures sorcery illness such as *odi* and *mata* through divine powers.

The *shashthrakarai* among the Yerava designates cowrie pandit as well as magician. He plays an important role in diagnosing the illness, finds out the cause of other problems, by tying of amulets and curing illness caused on account of evil eye and fear.

The herbalists among the Yerava are called *Mardukarai.* This post is not hereditary but usually the sons are inducted in this profession. Usually, the sons develop interest and become successor. The *Mardukarai* is also not a full time herbalist. They treat almost all illness caused on account of wrong diet, climatic changes, accidents, injuries and physical one. The herbalists diagnose illness based on signs and symptoms and involve them in the preparation of medicine.

The *bethikarthi* among the Yerava is the traditional untrained midwife. They are by and large aged person, who acquired the art of conducting deliveries through their mothers/grandmothers or any other close relatives or through watching number of deliveries. People have more faith on bethikarthi than doctors and who prefer to conduct delivery at their house alone. Hence, almost all deliveries take place within their huts only.

Conclusion

The Yerava is a Scheduled Tribe of Karnataka, mainly settled in the Virajpet taluk of Madikeri district. The huts of Yerava are nucleus and usually built on a slope by leveling out the house site. One for lot of open space all around the hut which helps in getting sufficient fresh air and light. Also they are in the natural forest helps them a lot in gaining good health. The term 'health' for the Yerava is a state of 'full fitness', i.e., a healthy person has a good conditioned body and can carry out his routine work with full zeal. He can work hard and eat well. The attribution of some illnesses to certain deities, spirits, sorcery, fear and evil eye indicates that still the Yerava have not changed in their traditional modes of beliefs and practices related to health and illness.

The health status of the Yerava is concerned, they are no way exceptional compared to other tribes, though are very rich in the then ecology. Their health seeking behaviour and attribution of causative factors are more or less not changed drastically. They associate only during the working hours with the common people. The PHC is also situated about nine km from their settlement and visiting to the PHC is only during emergency and also on the weekly shandy day, forcimg them to depend on medical systems in confidence.

References

1. Bhat, H.K. 1989. Concept of health and disease among the phase of Meghalaya. Tribal Health - Edited by B. Chaudhuri New Delhi: Inter-India Publications, pp. 250-272.
2. ——— 1979. Ethno medicine in a Mysore Village. Unpublished Ph.D. thesis to the Karnataka University, Dharwad.
3. ———1976 Medicine men of Basavanahalli: A study of ethno medicine. Journal of Indian Anthropological Society, 11(1): 45-53.
4. ———1976. Spirit illness in a south Indian village. Bulletin of Anthropological Survey of India, 25(3 and 4), 73-84.
5. Brown, Peter J., Bruce Ballard, and Jessica Gregg 1994. Culture, Ethnicity and the Practice of Medicine. In An Introduction to Human Behaviour for Medical Students. 2nd Edition. Alan Stoudemire, ed. pp 84-106, New York: Lippincott.
6. Caudill, William 1953. Applied Anthropology in Medicine. Anthropology Today: An Encyclopedic Inventory. A.L.Kroeber, ed.Pp.771-806. Chicago: The University of Chicago Press.
7. Cassel, E.J, 1976. The healer's art: A new approach to doctor-patient relationship. New York: J.B. Lippincott Company
8. Census of India 1981. The Yeravas of Madikeri, Ethnographic Notes and Special studies on Scheduled Castes and Scheduled Tribes, Series-9, Karnataka, part XI.
9. Foster, G.M. 1978. Medical Anthropology, New York: John Wiley & sons, Inc.
10. Hahn, Robert A.1984. Rethinking "Illness" and "Disease" contributions to Asian Studies 18:1-23
11. ——1995 Sickness and Healing: An Anthropological Perspective. New Haven: Yale University Press.
12. Klienman, Arthur 1980 Patients and Healers in the context of culture. Berkeley: University of California Press.
13. Sedgwick, Peter 1981. Illness-Mental and otherwise. In Concepts of Health and disease: Interdisciplinary perspectives. Arthur L. Caplan, H.Tristam Engelhardt Jr., and James J. Mc.Cartney, eds.pp 119-30. London: Addison-Wesley.
14. Singer, Merrill and Hans Baer 2007. Introducing Medical Anthropology: a discipline in action, United Kingdom: Altamira press.
15. Whitaker, D. Elizabeth 2003. The Idea of Health: History, Medical Pluralism, and the management of the Body in

Emilia-Romagna, Italy. Medical Anthropology Quarterely17 (3):348-75.

16. Weaver, Thomas 1968. Medical Anthropology: Trends in Research and Medical Education. Essays on Medical Anthropology. T.Weaver ed. pp 1-12 Southern Anthropological Society Proceedings. No.1. Athens. Ga: University of Georgia Press.

2

The Bathukamma Heritage

— *Dr. D. Satyanarayana*

Bathukamma festival is a festival of flowers and is being celebrated with pomp and gaety across Telangana. It had been preserved only by oral/folk traditions until 18th century, when one Kanchanapalli Narasimharaju, the native of Mogilicherla of Warangal district, had written the inherited mysticism and the floral worth of the deity Bathukamma[1]. The floral deity is prepared by every Hindu woman in every village of Telangana. It finds invoked by teenaged girls and women with hymns and claps taking rounds around the goddess, arranged around a temporarily dug well at a courtyard in every street of every village. The celebration goes on for eight to nine days, varying from region to region, in the evenings only starting from Mahalaya Amavasya. Similar folk dances were found in *Teej* festival among the Lambadi tribals of Telangana and in Kaikottikal of Kerala, Kummi of Tamilnadu, Garja in Gujarat, Gangore in Rajasthan and Gondli/Gondhali in Central India.

The festival resembles that of "Phoolwalon kee siar" in Delhi's Mehrauli, where the dignitaries offer floral chaddars on pankha at the Dargah of Khwaja Bakhtiar "Kaaki". The public, irrespective of faith, community and caste, join the fare with qawwali on each day, besides sports competition - the kho-kho, kabaddi and patang baazi. The forcus shifts later to Yogamata Temple aside where the devotees continue the process like the dargah.

The term **Bathukamma** is the combination of words – **Bathuku** and **Amma** suggesting the mother floral deity is recognized as an enlivening goddess. Our life needs health and wealth. The deity safeguards them and enables the barren women begot issues and drougth-hit cultivators with bounteous harvest from heavy downpour. She has been eulogized as the consort of trio - Brahma, Vishnu and Siva as Saraswati, Sri Lakshmi and Parvati [Gauramma], the givers of knowledge, food and wealth, besides future respectively. A hymn dedicated to her eulogize as ***Srilaxmi nee mahimalu gauramma***

Chitramai tochunamma
Bharati sativayyai
Brahmakillaaluvai
Parameshu raanivayyee gauramma
Bhaaryavaitivi harikini

Meaning: O Goddess Srilaxmi! We feel strange at your mystic belief. You are Bharati, Sati, wife of Brahma, wife of Parameswara and became the wife of Hari (Vishnu).

Earlier, the deity Ellamma or Renuka was expected to confer such blessings. The idol of such goddess (Lajjagauri or Jogulamba) is found in Alamapur, Mahabubnagar district[3] and a few other places with flower in place of head, heavy breasts and widely opened *yoni* (female genital) indicating the expectations of the people from the deity – flowers, milk and crops/children respectively. Though the floral deity is recognized as the manifestations of various deities, she is invariably called Bathukamma by the rural folk of Telangana. They love the goddess so much that they named some of their villages after her name as Bathukeswaramu near Vadapally, Nalgonda district and Bathikepally, Karimanagar district.

Tracing History

Historians find it difficult to ascertain about the origin of worship about the deity. It is not so easy to trace out the origins of the goddess. Yet, some humble attempts were being made to know her historical evolution. Hala was one among the celebrated rulers of the Satavahana dynasty who was the first empire that ruled Telangana in between c. 80 BC and c. 230 AD[4]. His compiled work ***Gathasaptasati*** starts and ends with the eulogy of the goddess Gauri, the consort of Lord Pasupati[5]. Since all the important hymns of Bathukamma mention the name of Gauramma at the end of every line, it can be attributed the Bathukamma festival must have been in vogue from the Satavahana dynasty i.e. the dynasty from some 2,000 years onwards.

During the Ikshvaku kingdom, a deity called Hariti was invoked in Nagarjunasagar area for children and cattle. An area named Hariti Revula - Hariti Chalka was found in the Amrabad Mandal of Mahabubnagar district from where the successive dynasty of Chalukyas was deemed to have evolved[6]. The goddess Hariti appears to have been revered by the people analogous to Bathukamma. Madhava Varma, one of the greatest rulers of Telangana during 5th century AD in a traditional Bathukamma number mentioned the reason for the self-sacrifice of a young Vaisya caste girl Vasavambika. She was being attributed as Bathukamma and Vaishyas in Telangana treat her as the original goddess of Bathukamma[7].

After the rule of Chalukyas we come across the deities Padmakshi, Mahuramma, Ekavira, Mailamma, Kakati, etc., who were invoked by the Kakatiya rulers of Telangana. A clinching evidence of Bathukamma emerged during the rule of this dynasty. An inscription found in a village named Vadapally in Nalgonda district states that five brothers of Meluguntu lineage constructed a ***trikuta*** temple in Brathukeswaramu ***sthaana*** in the name of their sovereign Ganapatideva and their father Kode and mother Mailasani in 1211 AD donating 30 ***puttis*** of Velivolamu land towards the ***anga ranga bhogas*** and ***naivedya*** of the deities[8].

A famous Telugu scholar Arudra stated that the Bathukamma festival must have evolved during the reign of the Kakatiya ruler Rudramadevi (1262-89 AD)[9]. Another scholar Tirumala Ramachandra also wrote that she celebrated the Bathukamma festival after her victory over her brothers' kingdom of Yadavas of Devagiri, Maharashtra[10]. But the contemporary literature did not mention the word Bathukamma. And Jayapa Senani, who compiled the contemporary ***desi*** and ***maarga nrityas*** in his monumental work ***Nritta Ratnavali*** mentioned ***Bhillangana nritya*** which is similar to the ***Gondli nritya*** analogous to Bathukamma dance. In fact, the Bhillangana nritya is the one performed by Bhil tribes of the northern areas surrounding Telangana.

One more traditional Bathukamma number mentions another celebrated king of Telangana Ibrahim Padusha[12] who ruled from Golconda between 1550 – 80 AD. Though, he was a Muslim ruler, he was loved by his Hindu subjects so much that he was called by them as Malkibharama. A Hindu temple of a mother goddess has also been invoked by Hindu devotee's right from early Kakatiya times it was not demolished even by the Muslim rulers of the Qutbshahi dynasty, which needs to be appreciated. In other words, the Bathukamma sort of celebrations continued in Golcnda kingdom also upto seventeenth century.

The Golconda kingdom was succeeded by the Nizam State of Hyderabad (1724 – 1948), by then the folk tradition of Bathukamma festival became so popular that the scholars could not keep quiet without recording the traditional and new numbers. In this regard, we come across the poet Kanchanapalli Narasimhadasu, who recorded her history in some 33 stanzas in around 1750 AD. He belongs to Warangal belt, wherefrom the Kakatiyas have ruled and began the tradition of Bathukamma, what we witness today.

The scholars and poets galore since then went on focussing on the theme of Bathukamma. Kavisamrat Viswanatha Satyanarayana is the most famous Telugu poet and the first Telugu poet to receive Jnana pith award. Though, he was not the native of Telangana, but an Andhraite to have composed a much acclaimed poetic marvel entitled ***Kinnerasaani Paatalu*** in the style of a Bathukamma number, which runs "Srilaxmi nee mahimaloo gauramma..."[13].

The Flower Goddess Bathukamma

There are two types of Bathukammas – Boddemma, the small one and Saddula Bathukamma, the big one. Boddemma is prepared in circular and conical shape on a bamboo plate called ***Sibbi*** or metal plate called ***Tabuku,*** by the girls every evening from the day one of the Bathukamma festival until the last day when the Saddula Bathukamma is prepared by the women. Boddemma is prepared a height of half foot to one foot with flowers available in the backyard of the houses, whereas the Saddula Bathukamma is prepared in a height of one foot to four feet in a large circular metal plate called ***Taambalem*** with leaves as the base, on which variety of flowers were arranged in a conical shape in stepped up levels.

It is said in a Bathukamma song that ***theerokka puvvu*** i.e., each and every variety of flowers and ***nootokka puvvulu*** i.e., 101 varieties of flowers are used to decorate/ compose the Bathukamma. Yet, the yellowish flowers dominate Bathukamma since the colour symbolises turmeric/haldi, in turn symbolises the longevity of the husbands of those women. Therefore, the yellow flowers like ***Tangedu*** (tanner's cassia), Gummadi (pumpkin),

Beera (ridge gourd), Banthi (Marie gold), etc. are found predominantly in every Bathuakamma. The primary icon in every Bathukamma is Tangedu flowers, which were brought from nearby forests and meadows, especially by the men-folk of every family. A cat race among the collectors of the Tangedu flowers for the quantity of the flowers to make their Bathukamma look bigger than their counterparts. The apex body of the Bathukamma is decorated with a yellowish bud taken out of pumpkin flower which resembles a pole erected in a vessel representing Sivalinga, thence known as Gauramma , who is said to bless the humankind.

The Bathukamma is decorated with other important flowers like Katla (blue) representing the colour of Vishnu–Laxmi and Gunaka (white) representing the colour of Brahma - Saraswati apart from the yellow colours representing Gauri - Pasupati - the trinity with their consorts. The famous numbers on Bathukamma include the title numbers like "okkesi puvvesi chandamama..." (O moon, I am offering one flower each time...) and "ememi puvvoppune gauramma..." (O Gauri, which flower you cherish...) which reveal the predominant role of flowers in the decoration and celebration of Bathukamma festival[14].

The Celebrations

The Bathukamma celebration runs for eight to nine days, varying from region to region, from the Mahalaya Amavasya (New Moon day of Asvayuja Masa in Indian official lunar calendar). The first day is called the day of ***engili poolu*** when the boys of every street dig a circular well of one yard measure and well decorated with about 10 circular platforms of three inch height by the girls by that evening. The girls then bring their Boddemmas, keep them on the circular platforms and take circular rounds around the Boddemmas singing hymns in chorus to a leading singer in praise of the deity. A kind of rhythmic movement of body slightly slanting towards the

Boddemmas, while clapping in rhythm invariably found during their play. The numbers sung during the celebrations are called Bathukamma songs and every line of the number ends with either of the words ***uyyaalo, valalo, kol, gummadi*** (pumpkin), ***gauramma*** (goddess Gauri) and ***chandamaama*** (Moon). Hence, the nummbers are also called ***uyyaala paatalu*** (uyyaala numbers).

Such plays are repeated continuously for seven or eight days as per the traditions of the locality, leaving the sixth day called ***arrem***. On the final day, i.e., 8th or 9th day ***Saddula Bathukamma*** play is played by all the women and girls together with big and small Bathukammas and the lead is taken by the elderly women takes the lead. More time is taken on this day to sing many songs praising the goddess Bathukamma or her other forms Gauramma and Srilaxmi. Epic stories, local histories, famous incidents, etc. are also sung amidst villagers. The numbers were actually meant to educate the girls, boys and of course others on the cultural and moral heritage of the mankind to ensure better and happy living.

During the dusk of the last day, the bigger Bathukammas are finally invoked at the Bathukamma well and ferried on in procession by men of each family on their heads and shoulders to a nearby tank or stream or river amidst the sounds of musical instruments (***dappulu***) and Bathukamma songs. Once again, the womenfolk play the Bathukamma numbers on the bank of the river or the tank and then immerse the Bathukammas in the waters of the river or tank beseeching the goddess Gauri to come immediately next year. The trend follows the tradition of ***vaayinam*** wherein the women use to exchange the sweet flour (***sattu***) prepared with the new crops of maize, green gram or millets saying ***ichchuko vaayinam*** (give me yours) and ***puchchuko vaayinam*** (take mine). The villagers then return to houses. The next day in some villages or the second day in other villages is celebrated as Dasara festival with consumption of liquor and non-vegetarian food with varieties of snacks. That evening, the village men and boys go to a nearby ***Shami*** (***jammi***) tree and distribute its leaves as the gold, amongst the people wishing each other for better future.

On the eve of the festival, every household in Telangana invite their newly married and recently married daughters with husbands and new born children and buy new clothes for all of them. It is treated as a prestigious issue in the villages. It is understood that the new crops enable the households to celebrate the flower festival amidst pomp and gaeity.

The Bathukamma festival is the biggest in Telangana and hence the people of Telangana used it as a symbol for unity and united means of strength during their struggle for separate state of Telangana during the two decades recently. This is the reason why the new government of Telangana made the Bathukamma as the official festival of the state and celebrated it in a grand manner with ten crore of rupees. Further, it made the Tangedu (Tanner's Cassia) flower as the state flower and the Shami (jammi) tree as the state tree.

References

1. B. Ramaraju. 1968. ***Telangana Palle Paatalu*** (Telugu). Hyderabad: Author. p. 75.
2. *Op.cit.*, pp. 76-77.
3. M. Radhakrishna Sarma. 1972. ***Temples of Telingana.*** New Delhi: Munshiram Manoharlal Publications Pvt. Ltd. Pl. 106.
4. For details, see P. V. Parabrhma Sastri. 1992. ***Satavahana Epoch – A New Light.*** Hyderabad: Telugu Goshti.
5. See R. G. Basak. 1974. ***Hala's Gathasaptasati***. Calcutta: Asiatic Society of Bengal.
6. Author's visit.
7. B. Sujata Sekhar. 2005. ***Telangana Bathukamma Paatalu – Samajika, Samskritika, Bhasha Pariseelana*** (Telugu). Devarakonda: Samskritika Sahiti Samakhya. p. 30.

8. N. Venkata Ramanayya. 1994. ***Inscriptions of Andhra Pradesh – Nalgonda District.*** Vol. II. Hyderabad: Government of Andhra Pradesh. pp. 106-108.
9. See Arudra. 2005. ***Samagrandhra Sahityam*** (Telugu). Vol. I. Hyderabad: Telugu Akademi.
10. Tirumala Ramachandra. 2013. ***Andhra Veerulu*** (Telugu). Hyderabad: Emesco. p. 32.
11. See Jayapa Senani. 2010. ***Nritta Ratnavali*** (Telugu). Hyderabad: Telugu University.
12. See ***Telangana Bathukamma Paatalu. Op.cit.*** p. 20.
13. See Viswanatha Satyanarayana. 2011. ***Kinnerassani Paatalu*** (Telugu). Hyderabad: Viswanatha Sahitya Peetham.
14. Chintapalli Vasundhara Reddy. 1986. ***Telugu Janapada Sahityamu – Streela Geyamulalo Sampradayamu*** (Telugu). Hyderabad: Telugu University. pp. 446 – 451.

3

Intangible Cultural Heritage of South India

— G. Suryanarayana

Introduction

The origin and establishment of Hinduism dates back to Vedic period or beyond. Since then, temples became the centers of learning and wisdom. Religious, spiritual, social, economic and traditional aspects of lives of the people were incorporated in formulating and continuing the temple traditions.

They became monumental institutions to preserve the cultural and spiritual heritage of India forever. The temples may be called living museums of our traditions designed to elevate mankind.

The present paper is focused to highlight "The Intangible Cultural Heritage" being observed by the devotees at famous Simhachalam Temple in Andhra Pradesh.

Simhachalam Temple.. Intangible cultural heritage of Simhagiri Hills, Visakhapatnam, Andhra Pradesh

Simhachalam Temple is situated on Simhagiri Hills, 18 Kms. away from Visakhapatnam city on Eastern Ghats at a height of about 250 mtrs. above the sea level. The presiding deity is Varaha Lakshmi Narsimha combining the iconography features of Varaha and Narsimha. The image resembles a Sivalingam covered with sandal wood paste. Once in a year during 'Chandanotsava' day (VaisakhasuddhaTadiya), the entire sandal wood paste is removed and the 'nijaroopam' of lord is seen by pilgrims. Again the nijaroopa is covered with fresh paste. Similarly, the paste will be smeared thrice a year.

As per legend, this temple recounts the great devotee Prahalada and his demonic father 'Hiranyakashapa'. Prahalada being a devotee of lord Narayana, expressed his devotion towards Vishnu. Since Hiranyakashapa disliked his son's devotion towards Vishnu, he became infuriated. He made several attempts to kill Prahalada like throwing him off a mountain top, putting him into chamber of snakes and throwing him into a cage of a hunger tiger. Vishnu rescued Prahalada from all these evil acts. While throwing a mountain top over Prahalada, the lotus feet of lord Narayana sunk into the earth at this place. As per the request of Prahalada, the lord then assumed the form of Varaha – Narsimhadeity here.

As per historical inscriptions dated far back to 1098 AD, the Chola king Kulothunga provided some clues to its antiquity. Another inscription depicted the Queen of Kalinga (ancient Orissa)(1137-56 AD) of covering the image with gold, while a third inscription depicted the eastern Ganga king of Orissa, Narasimha Deva built the main shrine in 1267 AD.It has been hailed as the most famous and the best sculptured shrine.

Shri Krishna Deva Raya (Vizianagara King) after defeating the Gajapati ruler of Orissa Gajapati Prataprudra Dev, visited the shrine twice in 1516 AD and 1519 AD and offered numerous villages for maintenance along with valuable jewellery of which emerald necklace is still in temple. The royal family of Vizianagaram, Pusapatis' have been the temple trustees.

Devout pilgrims have their heads tonsured as a sort of offering to the Lord and have a holy bath in Gangadhara stream and enter the temple for darshan. After the darshan, devotees pledge near the Kappa Stambham (Pillar) for fulfillment of their much cherished wishes.It is widely believed that this pillar had the miraculous power to cure diseases and provide barren women with fertility. Many childless couples embrace the Stambham with the belief of getting the bliss of parenthood. Thus, this divine pillar attracts lot of devotees with the hope of realizing their dreams.

Several rituals are being performed in this temple every day from early morning till late night. The major festivals are being performed in the temple among Chandan Utsavam being the major event of the year. Thousands of people from round the world, particularly from the coastal states of Andhra Pradesh, Orissa, Karnataka and Tamilnadu visit the temple to take the darshan of the lord in his true form.

The present paper is being aimed to highlight the intangible cultural heritage being observed by the devotees at Simhachalam Temple.

Visakhapatnam is the shore based city surrounded by Eastern Ghats in the northern districts of Andhra Pradesh and is also known as *the City of Destiny.* It is well connected by road, rail and air with a number of large and medium Industries including gigantic Steel Plant.

Eastern Naval Command has its headquarters based in the city. It also has an attractive tourist importance. The city has various religious and cultural heritage sites.

Simhachalam Temple is situated on the Eastern Ghats at the height of 250 mts above sea level. near Visakhapatnam. It is one of the famous Vaishnava Temples of our Country. The presiding deity is being "Varaha Lakshmi Narsimha Swamy", an incarnation of lord Vishnu. The importance of the temple is that lord Vishnu blessed 'Prahlada' in the form of 'Tribhanga', a posture like Varaha, Nara and Simha known as Varaha Narasimha who killed 'Hiranyakasyapa' in two of the Avataras of lord Vishnu. Here, the moolavirat finds covered with sandal wood paste.

The nijaroopa of the lord is seen once in a year i.e., "Vaisakhasudda Tadiya" and smeared with sandal wood paste thrice a year. The paste is offered to soften the Ugravatara (fierce anger) of the lord. We witness many intangible heritage activities being affirmed by the devotees in this temple. A holy bath in the '**Gangadhara**' water flowing from hill top with rich herbal perfumes that they believe purifies the body and mind to worship the God.

Dwajastambham is installed for identification of the Lord inside the temple. The unique importance of this temple is that the lord facing idol surrounding towards West unlike many other temples. West facing bestows the sign of victory.

At the Lotus feet of God - Devotees with tonsured head bowing to the Almighty, the belief to devoid all passions of life with total surrender in absolute faith.

Devotees from remote and rural areas, mostly in groups along with Gurus, visit the temple and perform rituals before entering the main Ttemple.

Moolavirat - 'VarahaLakshmi Narsimha' A replica is seen here along with nijaroopa posture. The devotees offer their vows for a long, healthy, wealthy, and prosperous life.

The **Chief Priest** of the Temple Shri Mortha Sitarama-charyulu has been the chief priest of the temple for over 45 years and has conducted many important rituals and festivals including 'Chandana Utsavas'. Devotees feel himself as a bridge between themselves and the Almighty.

Preparation of Sandal wood paste – The paste is prepared which is applied to the Moolavirat thrice in a year. The total quantity of sandalwood paste covered on Moolavirat is about 480 kgs (half a tonne). It is a common belief that doing so cools down the anger of the 'Ugra Narasimha'.

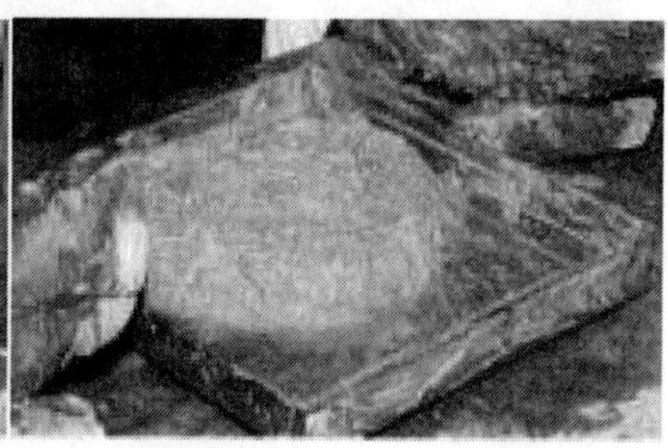

Mangala Harathi given to the Lord by the Priest will be offered to the Devotees with the belief to focus the mind on the God for self purification. The Harathi also clears the environmental air pollution in the Sanctum Sanctorum.

Shadhagopyam - Shadhagopyam to the devotees is believed to be the blessings of Lord for their vows.

Kappa Stambham is one of the pillars of Tribute. It means many devotees take oaths to come to this temple and make their offerings for the fulfillment of their much cherished wishes. It is believed that this pillar has the miraculous power to cure diseases and provide fertility to the barren women.

Ardent devotee with his tonsured head smeared with sandal wood paste and traditional namam on his forehead offering prayers to the lord for longevity with prosperity in front of Kappa Stambham.

Rich heritage and Architectural marvel on the outside walls of *sanctum sanctorum* of lord Narsimha and Varaha represent the Dravidian and Odissi cultures.

Ashirvachanam (The blessings from the God) The divine blessings to the devotees with temple honours in Mahamandapam in full satisfaction of their achievements and prayers.

Naamam: Hinduism is traditionally defined as the way of life and not a religion. *Naamam* on the forehead of hindus indicates the Sect and Caste. These marks vary from place to place. The Naamam or Vibhuti either vertical or horizontal hold a value of supreme importance for every hindu.

Rest a while ! After all the offerings and blessings, it is customary to rest for some time in the temple premises to recapitulate vows for purification.

Teppostavam Every year after the *Kalyanotsavam*, Lakshmi Narsimha Swamy is taken in procession in the Streets of Simhachalam village in chariot and in a decorative boat in the Pushkarani. Devotees ascend and have holy bath in Pushkarani with the belief of atoning for their sins.

The pilgrims from neighboring places and states gather near the temple and spend a night by singing bhajans and prayers in praise of the lord and anxiously wait for *nijaroopa darshan* on **'Chandana Utsava' day.**

4

Kheddasa Ritual of Tulunad

— Dr. H.K. Bhat and Dr. S.B. Konale

Tulunad, is a region in coastal Kerala and Karnataka extending from Kasaragod district in Kerala to Dakshina Kannada and Udupi districts in Karnataka. Fieldwork for this anthropological study was done during 2011-2014. However, data were collected for several years since both authors hail from the same region.

Tulunad region has its own agricultural calendar. Many rituals are observed during the cultivation, especially with reference to paddy cultivation. Paddy is the most important crop from the ritualistic point of view. It is also the staple diet of the people.

Keddasa is a land and cultivation related ritual of Tulunad. *Keddasa,* also known as *Keddeso, Keduvasa* and *Kedvasa* is observed on 27th, 28th, 29th and 30th days of the month of *Puyinthel* or *Ponni,* the tenth month of the Tulu Calendar. Uggappa Poojari who calls it *'Keddosa'* writes, *'Keddosa' panda Tuluvappe, Bhumi devi madmala a punind nambike.* It means that by *Keddasa* the people of Tulunad believe that the Tulu mother, the mother Earth is becoming *madmal.* In Tulu *'madmal'* means bride. But becoming madmal means attaining puberty or undergoing the monthly menses. Tulu Nighantu gives the meaning of

Keddasa as “A three day festival of Tulunad in the month of February. (There is a belief that the mother Earth blooms during these days and becomes fertile.....) The rituals connected with the cultivation begins with the beliefs and notions about the Earth or the land considered as mother nourishing living creatures which are her offsprings. A Sanskrit verse recited by many in India including the people of Tulunad, on rising from the bed in the early morning and before retiring to the bed during night addresses the Earth as Vishnupathni meaning ‘the wife of Vishnu’, who is clothed with the sea, bearing the mountains as breast, and begs pardon from her for touching her with feet or placing one’s feet on her. The puranic concept of Shri Devi, the Goddess of wealth, Lakshmi and Bhoodevi, the Earth Goddess being the two consorts of the God Vishnu is very much a part of the contemporary Tulunad beliefs.

The dance dramas known as Aata is being played by the artist troupes known as ‘Dashavatara melas sponsored by and affiliated to puranic deities, on the stages created in the open fields (for this reason these performances are also known as *bayalaata*. It means *aata* played in the *bayalu*, or the plain fields) depicting the puranic themes as the main means, medium and force in the process of enculturation, which has transmitted the belief through generations of people in this region. One could see that even an illiterate person in the region is adept in puranic knowledge. Once the Earth is regarded as the universal mother, the notion of femininity of the Earth naturally accompanies with it. Menstruation is the symbol of fertility associated with feminity. There is a belief that the Mother Earth also undergoes menstruation. The ritual of Keddasa is woven around this notion of menstruation of the mother Earth.

Palthadi Ramakrishna Achar, a scholar in Tulu culture has written a booklet on *Keddasa* under the title *Kedvasa* wherein he makes an analysis of the rituals. He has devoted a chapter for discussion on the term Keddasa, Here he disagrees with the explanation of the word based on its association with hunting associated with Keddasathe A definition is being given by Amrita Someshwar who has traced the origin of the word in Kheda, Khedda or Kedda meaning hunting in Kannada. The explanation of the term as 'tadbhava' form of 'Kadvasah' of Sanskrit given by Vighneshwar Sharma is acceptable to him. But, he does not endorse the concept of infertile or defective blood symbolizing menstruation, as the meaning of *vasah* in this context. He agrees with Povappa Kaniyuru, that Keddasa is being derived by the combination of 'kedu' and 'vasa', meaning miserable life indicating the restrained life of a woman during menstruation.

Finally, he points to the use of the term "kedvasa" used in holiday notices in schools, as well as in almanac and explains that Keddasa is derived by the substitution of 'ta' for 'da' in the process of combination of 'ketta' and Avasa, It means miserable life or living, indicating the practice of living in sheds, outhouses and sometimes in open yards and restrictions on taking meals in the night, chewing betelnuts and touching others during the menses period. On Keddasa day, her suffering increases,as she is expected to fast and see her *enjalu* or *made* does not fall on ground. She has to keep the banana or betel nut leaf on which she takes any food on the branches of some trees, to be thrown away only after keddasa.

Though, the real meaning of a word lies in its usage more than its etymological derivation and explanation, Achar's explanation is significant for its description of practices connected with the menstrual pollution of women practised during 'Keddasa', when the Mother Earth is under notional menstruation. The attitudes, behaviours and understanding of the happening in one's environment of common man are determined more by one's belief rather than the logical or linguistic explanations. Therefore, the whole complex of the behavior of common man, including the rituals is based on one's belief.

These beliefs give meanings to words and decides about the attitudes and behaviours, towards the real or notional phenomenon represented by the words.

During the field work, it was found that the people interviewed regarding *keddasa* among all castes in the two villages of Mittabegilu and Mala, and a cross-section of them in the two districts, believe that the Mother Earth undergoes menstruation during the period of Keddasa. Even a few people, who are considered as intellectuals and claim them to believe only in scientifically proved facts and call the belief about the Earth's undergoing menstruation is only a myth and superstitions agree that the people believe in it is a fact. Thus, they were unanimous on the meaning of *Keddasa* as the days of the menstruation period of Earth.

We could not get any definite answers about the origin of observance of the *Keddasa* in Tulunad either from among common folks or scholars and researchers. The people say that the practice is there from time immemorial.

Though, they could not give any evidence for the ordeal, the ethnic astrometeorological symbolism of the days is very significant. The nature gives a deserted look in winter by shedding leaves. As the winter gives way to the spring the plants come to life again with leaves, flowers and fruits; as if the Earth is delivering new babies. A woman bears children only after attaining puberty, indicated by menstruation. Therefore during this transitional period between winter and spring, the Earth is said to undergo menstruation, symbolizing the maturation and fertility of the Earth. Further, it is believed that the wind blowing from the east during this period is believed to be conducive to the lush growth of the greenery and blooming of flowers and bearing fruits in the fruit bearing trees. The absence or distrurbance in this wind is expected to cause crop failure, destruction of crop etc.

On the *Keddasa* day, people don't work dig the ground. They completely refrain from agricultural or horticultural operations. A oral message finds transmitted through generations about the bleeding trauma of Mother Earth when someone dug the ground . The digging of earth as such is being considered as the sinful act according to those informants.

Keddasa is observed generally for three or four days beginning from the evening of 27th of the *Ponni* month. On the first day, the house and the yard in front of the house is cleaned and purified using cowdung emulsion. A place in the yard, usually near the Tulasi *Katte*, is cleaned by removing litters scattered. The place finds purified by cowdung emulsion and made ready for the worship of Mother Earth. A big circle or square is then drawn on the purified spot with *'jedi mannu'* a kind of white clay found in Tulunad. Palthadi and Diva Kokkada have mentioned the use of *vibhuti* or sacred ash at some places for drawing the circle or square; Then a Kodi in plantain leaf with tip infact is placed on a *thadpe* and kept in the middle of the circle/square. The place *'nanyari'* or *'kudvari'* on that leaf.

Nanyari is a special type of sacred snack prepared only on the occasion of Keddasa. Rice is roasted accompanied by sprinkling of little salt water. Similarly *'kudu'* (horse gram), *enmell* (sesame) *avare* (seeds of a kind of beans), *padenji* (green gram), *kadale* (bengal gram) and *urd* (black gram) are also roasted, separately. These pulses are taken in equal quantity and roasted rice equal in quantity to all those grams are taken together. The roasted materials are then ground in the traditional grinding stone known as *'beesukallu'*. The *beesukallu* consists of two circular etched stone parts. A lower round flat stone of about three to five inches of thickness and a diameter of about one to one and half feet with a central wooden handle or axle. Another round flat stone with a central hole is placed on the lower stone by inserting its central handle through the central hole of this upper stone. This upper stone is fitted with a wooden handle towards its periphery. The grains are put around the central handle from above the upper stone. Then the upper stone is rotated by holding its lateral handle. The grains slowly move down, and get crushed between the two stones. The pulverised grains fall down aside. The whole apparatus is generally placed on a '*thadpe*'.

This coarsely powdered grains are mixed together adding dry coconut kernel gratings and jaggery. Some add bananas also. This mixture is known as 'nanyari' Ari(rice) and *kudu* (horse gram) are considered to be the most essential ingredients of nanyari. When only *kudu* and *ari* are used, it is known as '*kuduari*' when one cannot get kudu only roasted rice is used.

They keep a clean white cloth, *gejje kaththi* (a kind of sickle with hanging tiny jingling bells) and a green *madala kaddi* (rib of coconut leaflet). After placing them, things were offered to the Mother Earth with prayer, on folded palms (this posture is known as *Kaimugipune*). According to Ramakrishna Achar, some people keep leaves of *Taroli,* a small oil pot, the powder of the bark of *Baage* tree and seege seeds, and a bundle of handful *Karikke* grass. The lady who keeps these things takes oil from the pot and drops on the ground three times with the help of the Karikke grass and prays to the Mother Earth to go and take bathe in the river.

The *nanyari* is distributed to all. All eat *nanyari,* specially children relish it very much. It is said to be almost obligatory for the elder children to eat nanyari.

A kind of curry known as *koddel* or *gasi* using brinjals and drumsticks is prepared for the lunch. *Ajaine* a kind of fried side dish of *gujje* (tender jackfruits) is also prepared on the occasion.

Unpu is taken with curries during lunch (midday meal). During the night, the people do not eat *unpu.* They prepare some *adye* (snacks). Eating snacks made of wet ground rice is a convention. *Gatti* is made by steam cooking the wet ground rice packed in small leaf cups of banyan leaves. Some pack it in turmeric leaves and steam cook. Besides they may prepare *dose, adye* or *dose* being eaten by dipping or soaking in the coconut kernel juice, called *thaaraaida per* (coconut milk), in common parlance, sweetened by dissolving jaggery . Payasa or pudding of *rotti* is made by making *rotti* of *bolanthe ari* first and boiling it in *taraida* per with jaggery.

The second day of Keddasa is known as *nadu Keddasa* meaning middle *Keddasa.* Traditionally the main feature of nadu *Keddasa* is hunting. The rituals of *Keddasa* on being performed at the family level particularly by a muttaide, meaning, a married woman with a living husband, the hunting is mainly men's affair performed at the community level. Earlier the people (men) belonging to Nalike community used to go round the village, dressed in special costume. Wearing anklets known as *gaggara* (normally used in bhootha dances and announcing the forthcoming Keddasa and the hunting to the accompaniment of beating tembare (a kind of traditional musical drum).

They used to announce that women should go for hunting with *onake* (pestles used for pounding rice) and *kail* (the long spoons used for serving food).

They were asked to haunt for the games in the narrow valleys and the footsteps of ways of animal movement. The men were asked to stay back grinding rice and baking *dose.* Palthadi interprets it as a joke. Some say that it might be a joke, reminiscent of a probable earlier practice, though no historical evidence of hunting by women in Tulunad is available. Of course, in the history of Karnataka, we find the queens who braved to fight the armed forces of Aurangazeb and the mighty British, like Keladiya Chennamma and Kittoora Rani Chennama. Onakeya Obavva is a historical figure, who had alone killed many soldiers of Hyder Ali using *onake*. Rani Abbakka of Tulunad had fought with the Portuguese.

But at a pragmatic level, it seems to be hitting at the ego of the men who have given up the hunting mode of living and taken to sedentary cultivation. It is meant to arouse the militant adventurous spirit in men by asking them to do the opposite. Imposing feminity on men by asking them wear bangles and saree to arouse their masculinity, when they exhibit timidness and cowardice. It is a common dialogue observed during discourses in the community.

Sundar Kenaje in his folklore study of paddy growing stretches the significance of hunting during *Keddasa* too far in his analysis of its social relevance bringing in a gender conflict in his interpretation. He says it as an exhibition of masculine power before feminine meekness. Further, he says that this exhibition of masculine power by weakening the Earth is an indirect attempt to destabilize the women of a mother dominant or matriarchal community of Tulunad by influencing her. He insists the men go for hunting because women admire and like men who prove their ability by hunting. Then referring to the popular belief of the Tuluva people that the *Keddasada gaali* (the easterly *wind* of *Keddasa*) impregnates the flora, interprets the observance of Keddasa as a process of destabilisation of the matriarchal social system of Tulunad. But we do not find here any attempt to destalibilize the matriarchal social system. The observation of Keddasa is a part and parcel of the matriarchal socio-cultural mileu.

But, the explanation of Ashoka Alva, wherein he quotes and agrees to be more realistic, in the organized hunting expedition to prevent the destruction of crops by wild animals. The same idea is reflected in Peter Claus's explanation of annual hunting expedition of Kings, as an exercise for the prevention of such attack on farm lands by wild animals, and the productivity of nature by utilizing the excessive production as food surrounding Diva Kokkada, who refers to the above idea of Peter, quoted by Navada in one of his article. He tries to interpret the Keddasa hunting from the insider's view point, when he says the belief of *Tuluvas* that the bones would be weakened, if meat is not taken during *Keddasa* as the cause of practicing hunting, as a tradition.

With the enforcement of many wild life protection acts since independence, and the massive deforestation around the cultivated lands by enterprising people, and the population pressure, one seldom finds the people going for hunting any major games during Keddasa. But till recently people were found hunting even minor games like some fowls [*pundadakoli*] which could be hid in the bushes near the streams. People are also seen catching crabs or tortoise, and catching fishes by using different devices. They do this to fulfil the ritual needs as they believe in that ritual obligation of hunting and eating meat. Lately, many have given up hunting altogether and have restricted to eating meat of the domesticated birds or animals.

Though hunting is not practiced now, it is interesting to note the informations given by some old men of earlier practices, were noted by some authors in their works. There is nobody in Tulunad who had seen hunting with bows and arrows. As the memory of even very old people, they could only remember hunting using guns. Earlier people were using guns to fill the ammunition and make it secure with the help of a rod. This type of gun was known *mardda bedi*. *Mard* means medicine and *bedi* means gun. Guns in which cartridges are used are known as *Thotebedi*. People who used to hunt with guns are called '*Eeddu deepunakl*'. These gunmen used to stand in strategic positions. The others used to chase the animals by shouting and beating the bushes with sticks accompanied by barking dogs. They used to keep sickles, swords and spears armed. Some used to carry sand in the bags and throw into the bushes, or beat drums known as *dolu* or empty tins. The gunmen used to aim at the fleeing animals and shoot .

Once they were sure the animals were completely dead or unable to move the fraternity surround the animal. The skin is pulled off. The first share goes to the one, who shot it first. The one who has actually killed gets three shares consisting of the head, limbs and the waist. The remaining people get one share each. Even the dogs have their shares. The persons who made announcements about hunting in the village also gets his shares. Important persons like the *patels* and *gurikars* (headmen) of the village also used to get their shares, even if they could or did not participate in this collective hunting expedition.

An important ritual part of this exercise was the offering of the hunted animals liver to *bhootha* of the forest by putting it in fire.

Though, the practice of hunting is almost disappearing, cooking and eating meat dishes is practiced with the spirit of fulfilling a ritual obligation during *Keddasa* days, especially on the *nadukeddasa* day by the people belonging to meat eating castes. People belonging to those castes with vegetarian food habits do not observe this; But some prepare steam cooked adye or gatti of a mixture of rice and black gram. Some of them told our investigators that the black gram is a vegetarian counterpart of meat. They say it is called *maasham*' in Sanskrit, sounding almost like '*mamsa*' meaning meat. In this way, substituting meat by black gram they try to participate in this part of *Keddasa* ritual in spirit. Of course, they also generally prepare drumstick and brinjal curry. It may be noted that on other sacred occasions, like *pooje* and *homa* and the socio - religious rituals like marriages etc., drumsticks are not used in cooking.

The most significant part of the Keddasa ritual is observed on the last day. It is the day the Mother Earth is deemed to have her purificatory bath similar to the purificatory bath taken by women after two or three days of segregation during menstrual ordeal. While *Braahmana* observe it on the fourth day of Keddasa falling on the *Kumbha sankramana* (Maghi Sankranti), the day, when the sun passes to the Aquarius sign of zodiac, the non-*Brahmana* observe these rituals on the third day.

The rituals are observed by women, generally the eldest married women, with her husband alive. This performer of ritual rises up early in the morning and finishes her morning wash. She may not take a full bath. She then comes to the place, which was cleaned earlier and purified by applying cowdung. There she places generally seven leaves of Tarolu, with tips pointing to the west. Then they keep oil, cowdung, charcoal, *seege seeds, baage* bark powder, turmeric, *kumkum* and sandal paste. When *Tarolu* leaves are crushed inside water the water turns sticky. In the local language, they call it *'gompu'. Gompu* is used as a shampoo for cleaning hair by people of Tulunad. *Erpe* and *Bellante* leaves which were used to make *gompu* are used in place of *Tarolu.* The women of Tulunad normally do not wash hairs every day. They do once in a week, fortnight or month. When they do, they generally use the *gompu* as the exercise is obligatory when observing any *Vratha,* or perform any sacred performances. Similarly, the washing of hair is obligatory in a purificatory bath after menstrual ordeal. Keeping this *gompu* forming leaves is indicating this obligatory washing of hair. Earlier, the people did not use soap for bathing. They used powder of *Seege* - soapnut seeds, or the powder of *Baage* bark. *Baage* bark powder is coarse and acts as a scrub also. Seege seed powder produces lather like soap. One can find men and women using seege seed and Bage bark powder in their daily bath in Tulunad, through their number is small. The clothes worn on the body like saree and blouse and the ones used as bed sheets and coverings while sleeping should not be brought inside home after the purificatory bath without washing it or atleast symbolically washing it by wetting with water. Before the washing soaps and detergents became popular, the people used to soak the clothes in water after producing lather using soap nuts. Even now in the villages one can find the use of soap nuts known as *norekayi* [the liver literally mean the lather producing nuts). It was found that in some houses they keep soaps and detergent tablets, instead of *Seege, Baage* and purficatory bath.

Putting turmeric into water for bathing is the practice in women's purificatory bath.

Turmeric is often used esentially. Its medicinal and cosmetic value is recognised by modern pharmacy and cosmetic industries. It finds evidenced by the pharma-cosmetic products like turmeric creams being sold every where. Oil is used for applying to the body and hair before the bath and the hair after drying hair after the bath. Therefore, the oil is also offered. Mirror, and combs are also kept by some people.

The women under menses clean the floor, where they sleep during the period, using coconut husk, charcoal and cowdung before going for taking purificatory bath among the *Braahman*, who finds segregated into backyard. Hence, they keep cowdung and charcoal and paaleda kadddi. The woman first apply sandal paste and *kumkum* and sandal paste. Some have reported of keeping a lamp, wooden mane and karimani [the black beeded necklace]

People of some communities like Nalike, used to visit the houses of the people of other caste, where they were given the special snacks prepared for Keddasa, and coconuts.

During the Keddasa days people seldom works connected with cultivation that they do not even water the plants. The people who are otherwise busy have ample time at their disposal, spend afternoon and evening in some traditional rural games or sports in Doodu (now called *Kabaddi*) Kuttidonne, Chendu (foot ball), coconut hitting and cock fights.

Palthadi has written that *kolas* are held for bhoothas at some places. Our team could not find any of *bhootha kolas* held on Keddasa day at the places we did our field work. Even elderly people told that there was no bhoothakola on Keddasa in their village.

The practice of not doing any cultivation or the work that needs to cut or dig the Earth is found in almost all the villages of Tulunad.

In brief, *Keddasa* observation is based on the belief that the Mother Earth suffers from the pangs of menstruation which is a symbol of fertility. The women observe it by cleaning a little space in the front yard and offering all the requirements of a purificatory bath: Hunting and meat eating is associated with the observance of Keddasa by non-vegetarian food consuming castes.

When we do not know the origin or the orginators of the rituals and the socioeconomic conditions prevailing at the time of the origin. It is very difficult to exactly pin point the objectives behind such ritual. Neither we had any clue available in any ancient texts with respect to the objective of observance. Under such circumstances, it can only be beating about the bush and simply making conjectures, if we try to impute motives on the persons or groups, behind the introduction of such rituals, if any. Therefore, it is better to know what motivates the people at present to continue the practice of such ritual. We have interviewed people of different strata, men, women, young and old belonging to different castes in the two villages and beyond Tulunad regarding their beliefs. They all believe in the motherhood of the Earth and on the femininity of Earth. Though, they do not believe in the anthropomorphism of Earth in its physical form, certain states and values of Earth. It is such belief which has made them believe in the menstrual cycle of the Earth. They were not being worried about the scientific proof, but many things, which we cannot comprehend through five senses. However, they fear the consequences of not complying to these beliefs, that doing any work physically to the Earth like digging or other acts may bring in misfortune like failure of crops or fall in the yield, but not worried about the originator of such beliefs.

They believe in continuing with the traditions. Some persons believe in the actual menstruation of the Earth. but support the practice of rituals as a cultural practice. They say that every culture has some special behaviors for which one cannot and need not find logical reasons or physical causes. They form the basis of the identity of culture. Therefore, to maintain the identity of the culture, one had to observe certain rituals as far as possible without any physical harm. A few persons, who claim themselves to be progressive, especially among those who did not study any physical sciences formally, but have studied literature or humanities or social sciences cash in on the creations of some groups to keep some sections of the communities under perpetual control for exploitation. But our interactions with the members of those sections of people revealed they were not motivated by any considerations of other sections of the community. For example, a writer whom we have referred earlier charges the people of the patrilineal system of Tulunad. On deeper investigation, it was found the majority of patrilineal communities as later immigrants, who have abandoned the practice from matrilineal castes.For example, the Havyaka *Braahmana* living in the adjoining Malnad or northern coastal regions abstain from *Keddasa,* while those living in Tulunad practice, except the hunting part. So, is the case of the Karada *Brahmana* and *Kota Brahmina.* Hegde and Marati Nayak, are immigrant patrilineal communities, not belonging to *Brahmana* Varna. They observe Keddasa while the people of their community outside Tulunad abandon. There were also patrilineal communities like Chitpawan, who have not yet taken up the practice, due to.their living in limited clusters. Again there is no evidence of the Tulu speaking communities forcing others to adopt the practice.

On asking some of the Brahmana scholars for the reason behind, they say that they believe in Rgvedic injuntion of adopting noble thought from all the corners of the universe and some of them say that it is Manu's injunction to adopt local customs when one migrates to other places if these practices do not affect their basic value system. But these common people cannot pinpoint these reference in Rgveda or Manusmrithi.

However anthropologists know that cultural diffusion is natural process, taking place following cultural contacts.

The association and relevance of *Keddasa* to agriculture and paddy farming is obvious that the femininity, and menstruation are directly linked to the concept of fertility of the land. People refraining from cultivation activities shows its relation to agriculture at least notionally eventhough it cannot be proved by evidence. The belief about the power of *Keddasa gaali* (wind of *Keddasa*) to produce furits and flowers also connects it to cultivation.

It is also related to paddy that in *nanyari*, the special sweet preparation specific to Keddasa, the most essential ingredient is '*ari*' meaning rice. Further the '*adye*' or the snacks prepared on the occasion have only rice as the or the main ingredient. In the same time, the ritual obligation of eating meat or its substitutes may point out to the nutritional deficiency of rice, necessitating protein complements.

After the people advanced to peasant stage from the food gathering and hunting stage of cultivation and took up sedentary, individual or family level agricultural enterprenuership, the ritualisation of hunting during *Keddasa*, would have worked naturally as a force strengthening the community solidarity, besides regulating the biodiversity equilibrium.

One most significant aspect of the values inherent in the belief and behaviors of Keddasa is the religious touch. The Tulu culture, which is a part of the wider Hindu culture finds divinity in every part of nature. It does not believe in the exploitation of nature. It believes in enjoying the gifts of nature with a sense of gratitude towards the Earth for the nourishment. Food including water, is considered to be a gift of the Earth, even after the people have changed from the stage of the gathering of the natural products, to sedentary cultivation. This idea of gift of nourishment elevates the Earth to the status of Mother whose primary mission after delivery is to nourish the child with her breast milk. Further, we also find the sense of one's responsibility to one's mother in fulfilling or maintaining her cultural practices, that, the materials used in purificatory bath to get rid of the menstrual pollution are offered. The practice of maintaining gender-based domains of activity is strictly adhered in only women observing the rituals connected with *Keddasa*, as menstruation and consequent purification are purely in female domain.

Thus rituals of *Keddasa* symbolizes, the worldview, the religious beliefs and the human values and the social relations of Tulu people with respect to the Earth.

Acknowledgement: Most of the data presented here were collected for the project titled 'Paddy growing culture in Tulunad region of Karnataka. The first author, the Principal Investigator of the project acknowledges the financial support of IGNCA, New Delhi, for conducting this study.

References

1. Achar, Palthadi Ramakrishna. "KEDDAVASA - Acharane Vishleshane", Sullia, Janapada Koodugattu 2007.
2. Bhat, Guruaja. *Studies in Tuluva History and Culture*; Kallinapura S.K. 1975.
3. 1. Bhat, Gururaj and Keshava Krishna Kudva, "TULUVA CHARI TRE" UJRE, Organising Com mitte, V ishwa Tulusammelana. 2009.
4. Dharmakur, Sullivan, *Land and Caste in South India* : Cambridge: Cambridge University Press, 1965.

5

The status of Sudugadu Sidda Women

— ***Inamdar***

Status of Women in India: The origin of the Indian idea of appropriate female behavior can be traced to Manu in 200 BC: "by a young girl, by a young woman, or even by an aged one, nothing must be done independent, even in her own house". India is a multifaceted society, where no generalisation could apply to the nation's various regional, religious, social and economic groups. Nevertheless, certain broad circumstances in which Indian women live affect the way they participate in the economy. A common denominator in their lives is that they are generally confined to home, with restricted mobility, and in seclusion. Other, unwritten, hierarchical practices place further constraints on women. Throughout history, women have generally been restricted to the role of a home-maker; that of a mother and wife. Despite major changes in their status elsewhere in the world, the norms restricting women at home are still powerful, defining appropriate activities for women. They are, by and large, excluded from political life, which by nature takes place in a public forum.

In spite of our reputation for regarding woman, besides treating her as goddess, history tells about her often being ill-treated. There was no equality between men and women. This is true of ancient, medieval and early modern times barring some revolutionary movements such as that of Basaweshwara, the 12th century, philosopher, who advocated equality, casteless society, status for women, and the betterment of downtrodden. Reform movements in the 19th and 20th centuries led by social reformers provided boost to women's legal status in India. Independence of India heralded the introduction of laws relating to women. The Constitution provided equality to men and women and protection to realize their interests effectively. Special laws were enacted to prevent indecent representation of women in the media and sexual harassment.

Anthropology

1. The Concise Oxford Dictionary. "Study of mankind especially of its societies and customs; study of structure and evolution of man as an animal."
2. Kroeber. "Anthropology is the science of groups of men and their behavior and production."

Four major fields of Anthropology

1. Biological anthropology: The study of the variations that exist in humans based on biology
2. Archaeology: The study of the past and present through materials
3. Cultural anthropology: The study cultures of living people, and ANY variations
4. Linguistic anthropology: The study of languages and ANY similarities and differences that lie within
   - Holistic
   - Biological Approach
   - Comparative
   - Fieldwork

What does holistic mean: looking at the WHOLE picture, taking information from every available source to better understand.

Biological Approach: examines how biology and culture affect each other. ex: race is usually a cultural term, but can also be used as a biological component. Examines distance between biology and race, culture and race.

Comparative: cross-cultural comparison focuses more on non-western non-industrialised groups.

Fieldwork: anthropologists collect data in the field, digging for fossils, interview people, and collect other data.

Branches of Anthropology

- Physical Anthropology
- Social-Cultural Anthropology
- Applied Anthropology
- Linguistics Anthropology
- Archaeology Anthropology

I have selected Archaeology Anthropology. What begins one of the sub divisions of Anthropology deals with the pre-historic culture of our ancestors? It tries to trace the pre-phases of modern civilisations. The main aim of this branch of Anthropology is to reconstruct the origin speech an adulation of culture. I have applied the theory of Archaeology Anthropology seeking information of the ancient culture.

Thus, without its help, one cannot study in totality.

Modus operandi

1. Observation method
    - Participant Observation
    - Non-participant Observation
    - Interview Method
2. Question Method
   (Sampling and Hypothesis)

The term *sudugadu* means burial ground and *siddha* means, one who have acquired the mystic power in the cremation ground is known as *sudugadu siddha.* Though, their mother tongue is Telugu, they communicate with the local people in Kannada. According to Census-1981, their total population was 7, 669. They are non vegetarian. The state government has built houses for some, but others live in their own houses, which were little moderate.

The nomadic people obtain the livelihood through a variety of occupations like begging, selling herbal and aurevedic medicines, acrobats, jugglery, fortune-telling, trading hunting and gathering by migrating from one place to another. Still most of them pursue tradional occupation. A small section of the *sudugadu siddha* own cultivable lands and involve in agriculture. Their migration pattern depends on a considerable extent on topography. Men use saffron or white-colored shirt and dhoti and turban covering head.

Forehead, arms and chest with sacred ash (vibhuti) and vermilion Rudrakshii beads and lingam adore their neck and carry a *jolige* (to collect alms) and an umbrella. They walk on the street by making bell sound and alms were collected in the service i.e., foretelling about the future of persons. They beg in the name of their deity *Siddappaji.* They seek alms by standing on a nail-footed stool in some busy places, fairs and festivals, they move from one place to another during harvest seasons. Often, their children accompany with the duty to caring luggage. They build their tents near temples or in the outskirts of village. They don't have any leaders.

The *sudugadu siddha,* also called *Adikesidda, Pakanati golla* and *Kadu papa* recall their migration from the state of Andhra Pradesh to Karnataka .

The status of **women in India** has been subjected to many great changes over the past millennia. From equal status with men in ancient times through the low points of the medieval period, to the promotion of equal rights equal by many reformers, the history of women in India has been eventful. In modern India, they have held high offices in India including that of the President, Prime Minister, Speaker of the Lok Sabha and Leader of the Opposition.

The total population of this community as per my census is 738 among them 353 males and 377 females.

POPULATION CHART ACCORDING TO 2015 CENSUS conducted by the researcher.

Particulars	***Total***	***Male***	***Female***
Total No. of Houses	**342**	-	-
Population	767	372	395
Child (0-6)	158	69	89
Schedule Caste	738	353	377
Other cast	37	19	18
Literacy	**56.36 p.c.**	55 p.c.	1.36 p.c.+
Total Workers	**508**	396	112
Main Worker	**358**	0	0
Marginal Worker	**150**	0	0

Geographical location

Venkatapura is a revenue village 21 kms away from Karnataka University in Dharwad.

It is in hilly Malnad coastal belt with fertile red soil and higher rainfall, undulating plains of maiden fall of 6" in an elevation of 2.300' above the sea level.

The district lying between 14° 17' to 15° 50' Northern longitude and 74° 42' to 66° Western latitude covers an area of about 1,3'738 sq kms. Dharwad has on undulating hill terrain of 783m above the mean sea level [MSL].

The city is also the district head quarters and twins cities [Hubli and Dharwad] are known for educational, financial and industrial hubs for northern Karnataka.

Dharwad is one of the major cities on the Mumbai-Bangalore railway line and on the Pune-Bangalore National Highway NH-4.

Climate

Annual average temperature is 22° c- 25° c. The climate is warm and dry. The temperature raises to 40° c [summer and fall down to 18° c in winter. The average rainfall in the village is 28.2' cm. The people identify three seasons in a year viz., summer ['*besige kala*'] rainy ['*Male gala*'] and winter ['*chali gala*'] seasons.The summer lasts between February and May, the rainy season lasts between June and September whereas the winter between October and January.

The flora

Neem, Mango, Jali and Tamarind were the flora.

The fauna

Cows [68], Bullocks [3], Buffalos [72[, Dogs [98], Cats [36], Goats [59], Hen [119] and Horses [04] were the fauna.

The crops

Jowar ['*jwala*'] cotton [*Hatti*'] groundnut ['*shenga*'] sugarcane ['*kabbu*'].

The Food Habits

The villagers eat thrice a day with breakfast ['*nashta*'] at 8 am; lunch ['*oota*'] at 2 pm; and dinner ['*oota*'] at 10:30pm.

Their meals consists namely of Roti [Rotti] or Rice [*Anna*] and vegetables [*Kayi palle*] cereals [*Byale*], are used to prepare tiffin like *Avalakki Uppittu, Sajjage* and *churmuri* are taken with tea [*chaha*].

Occasionally they prefer non- vegetarian menu and it consists of mutton [*Kuri mamsa*], chicken [*Koli mamsa*], fish [*Minina Mamsa*].

Faith

There are three castes with different status and individual differences, among Hindus and Muslims the status of women among sudugadusiddas, which is the subcaste among Hindu caste system.

The status of women

Historians claim that women enjoyed an equal status with men in ancient India. It is said of them educated, had a say in family matters, took important decisions of life and were free to choose their husbands. The ancient system of "swayamvara" is mentioned in holy scripts and epics. A woman in ancient India was respected and given due importance in the society. Child marriage was unheard of and many women were famous sages like Gargi, Maitreyi, etc.

Medieval period

Indian women's position in the society further deteriorated during the medieval period, when child marriages and a ban on remarriage of widows became part of social life in some communities.

Historical practices

Traditions such as Sati, Jauhar, and Devadasi among some communities were banned and are largely defunct in modern India. However, some instances of these practices were still found in remote parts. The purdah is still being practiced among some communities. Child marriage remains common in rural areas, although it is illegal under current Indian law.

Sati

Sati is an old, almost completely defunct custom among some communities, wherein the widow was immolated alive on her husband's funeral pyre. Although, the act was supposed to be voluntary on the widow's part, its practice is being forbidden by the Hindu scriptures in Kali yuga, the current aeon.

Jauhar

Jauhar refers to the practice of voluntary immolation by wives and daughters of defeated warriors, in order to avoid capture and consequent molestation by the enemy.

Purdah

Purdah is the practice among some Muslim communities requiring women to cover them conceal from males on their faces and form.

Devadasis

Devadasi is often misunderstood as religious practice in southern India, wherein women were "married" to a deity or temple. The ritual was well-established by the 10th century A.D. and became outlawed by 1988 in the country.

Sudugadu siddha

The sudugadu siddha, also called Telugu jangaina, Gombeyatadavaru, pakanati golla, kadu papa, Abike sidda and siddaru, now live in Karnataka, They recall their migration from Andhra Pradesh to Karnataka.

These were semi.-nomadic and are located in Hassan, Chikkamagluru, Dharwad and Mysore districts. Census 1981 puts their number as 13, 206 (6, 658 males and 6, 548 females). They were mostly found in the rural ares. Telugu is spoken within the family and kin group and Kannada with other community people. The Kannada script is used for writing

Men and women occasionally consume mutton, chicken and egg. Rice, jowar and ragi are their staple cereals; toor and urad are the pulses being used. Groundnut oil is used for cooking. Men occasionally consume alcoholic drinks and smoke beedis and cigarettes, chew betel leaves and tobacco, which is common even today. Thy wear a saffron-colored dhoti, shirt stretching from forehead to arms when they go out seeking alms.

The term *sudugadu* means a crematorium or burial ground and *siddha* connotes mystic power. Thurston [1909], quoting from the Mysore Census report, 1901, states that them being mendicants like the Jogis, whom they itinerate, to whom the *kulavadi,* who takes clothes of the deceased snd a fee for every corpse burnt paid something as acknowledging their overlordship. According to a myth, they were the descendants of *siddappa,* bought back to life by *basava* after the dead body was taken to the burial ground.

Marriage

The community follows endogamy and exogamy is being observed when practice exogamy. Of late, there has been an increase in the age at marriage. The *sudugadu siddha,* once having exogamous surnames like pattapari, sali, vibhati, pujari and golladhari etc,. Marriage with one's, father's, daughter, mother's brother's, daughter or elder sister's daughter is preferred. Junior sorority and junior levirate are permitted. Adult marriage is the norm and marriages are being settled through negotiation. Monogamy and polygamy are the usual form of marriage. Vermilion on forehead and the *thaali* were the symbols for married woman. A bride-price of Rs.100 is obligatory. Residence after marriage is patrilocal. Either spouse can seek divorce. Remarriage after divorce, desertion or the death of a spouse and junior sororate are permissible.

Family

Nuclear joint families predominate, male equigeniture is the rule of inheritance and the eldest son succeeds the hereditary position.

Birth

A pre-delivery ritual is being observed on the fifth or seventh month of her first pregnancy. She had to sit on a platform with new dresses brought from her natal house. She allowed to back to natal house after this ritual.

Naming ceremony

The naming ceremony is observed for the newly born child at the age of five or ninth month for a boy before one year. The Puberty ceremony is being observed at the onset of menstruation. The teenaged girl had to sit in a segregated room for seven days, and she will be given a ritual bath after when she wears new dress and allowed to enter the house with yava aarati with coloured rice sprinkled on her body.

Death

The dead body is buried and ancestors are worshipped once a year. During the rainy season, they stick to their villages: some of them, who have small pieces of land, grow vegetables, horse gram, beans, ragi, etc. The sudugadu siddha strongly disapprove those against traditional way of life, and believe them as outcastes.

The nomadic communities of Karnataka thus engage selves in earning livelihood through various sources - some of them are multiskilled people. Mere traditional occupation does not enable them find sufficient income for proper sustenance, mobilizing them to eke out livelihood through tertiary jobs .They have shared *sudugadu siddha associations* and *co-operatives* headed by the same community people for socio-economic development. The state government had several schemes for their amelioration and their wards were being extended boarding facilities.

Domestic violence

Domestic violence in India is endemic.Around 70 percent of women in India were victims, according to Renuka Chowdhury, former Union Minister for Women and Child Development.

The National Crime Records Bureau revealed some crime against a woman is committed every three minutes, a woman is raped every 29 minutes, a dowry death occurs every 77 minutes, and one case of cruelty finds committed by either the husband or his relative, every nine minutes. This occurs despite the fact that women were in legally protected from domestic abuse under the Protection of Women from Domestic Violence Act.

In India, domestic violence towards women is considered as any type of abuse that can be considered a threat; it can also be physical, psychological, or such abuse to any current or former partner. It is not handled as a crime or complaint; but seen more as a private or family matter. In determining about such complaints, it is based on caste, class, religious bias and race, which also determine whether action is to be taken or not. Many studies about the prevalence of such violence resort to criminal-justice approach, but most women refuse to report. These women were guaranteed constitutional justice, dignity and equality, but continue to refuse reporting in the sociocultural context.

Sanitation

In rural areas, schools have been reported to have access to improved sanitation. The girl students were forced ease selves in the open air, unlike boys. The lack of facilities at home forces the women to wait for the night to relieve selves and avoid being seen by others.

In 2011 a "Right to Pee" (as called by the media) campaign began in Mumbai, India's largest city. Women, but not men, have to pay to urinate in Mumbai, despite regulations against the practice. Women were sexually assaulted, while urinating in fields. Thus, the activists have collected more than 50, 000 signatures supporting their demands that local government stops charging women to urinate, build more toilets, keep them clean, provide sanitary napkins and a trash can, and hire female attendants. In response, city officials have agreed to build hundreds of public toilets for women in Mumbai, and some local legislators now promise to build such ecofriendly toilets in every district.

Child marriage

Child marriage continues even today. Historically, child brides would live with parents until they reach the puberty. In the past, child widows were condemned to a life of great agony, shaved heads, living in isolation, and being excommunicated by the very society. Although, the practice was outlawed [1860], it is still a common practice.

Education

Though, it is proliferating, the female literacy rate in India is less than the male literacy rate. Far fewer girls than boys finds enrolled in schools, and many girls drop out. In urban India, the girls were nearly on a par with boys in terms of education. However, in rural India, girls continue to be less educated than boys. According to the National Sample Survey Data [1997], the states of Kerala and Mizoram have approached universal female literacy. According to scholars, the major factor behind such improvements in the socioeconomic status of women in Kerala was literacy.

Social attitudes

- Social attitude to the role of women lags much behind the law. The attitude which considers women fit for certain jobs and not others, causes prejudice in those who recruit employees. Thus women find employment easily as nurses, doctors, teachers, secretaries or on the assembly line.

- Even when well qualified women are available, preference is being given to a male candidate of equal qualification. A gender bias creates an obstacle at the recruitment stage. Though the law proclaims equality, it is not always practiced, accounting for the gender-bias in recruitment.
- The in-built conviction that women were incapable of handling arduous jobs and were less efficient than men influences the payment of unequal salaries and wages for the same job.
- A woman could still bear with such problems, if she had control over the money she earns. But in most families, her salary gets handed over to the father, husband or in-laws.

Land and Property Rights

In most Indian families, women, rarely own any property in their name, and do not get a share of parental property. The enforcement of weak laws in their protection reflects them to have least access to land and property.

The Hindu Personal Laws - 1956 gave women rights to inheritance. However, the sons had an independent share in the ancestral property, while the daughters share finds based on that received by their father. Hence, a father could effectively disinherit a daughter by renouncing his share of the ancestral property, but the son would continue to have such share in his own right. After amendment of Hindu laws in 2005, women have been now provided an equal status to that of men.

Anomaly - 1

Lack of education and awareness, socio-economic

status, alcoholic abuse, one parent abusing another in presence of children are quite common.

Anomaly - 2

Physical effects – injury, loss of speech, aches and pain, burns, substance abuse, gynecological issues, sexually transmitted diseases, unintended pregnancy resulting in abortion, etc.

- Mental and emotional health problems – withdrawal, unsocial behavior, multiple sexual partners, insomnia, depression and several others can also result.
- Apart from this, when the knowledge of abuse reaches others in the community, abused women are often being shunned and forced to live in isolation. In many cases, women suffer silently for this very reason, the fear of consequences. They seldom realize the consequences of putting up unanticipated.

6

The Ecological and Cultural Heritage of Dange Dhanagars

— *Jayawant B. Ambekar*

Cultural process includes economic, ecological, religious and political aspects that are regulated by culture, which helps people to transform their environment, relate to one another to create meaning ensure their existence.

The economy and process of socio-cultural changes among the indigenous communities can be understood better in their cultural, ecological and economic contexts. Rather, a cultural-ecological perspective, I think is best suited to study jatis, communities and groups, possible to suggest appropriate alternative development strategies. (Ambekar, J.B. 2009: 19-31)

To understand the adaptation patterns of various communities, the method of cultural- ecology is a highly useful tool for the anthropologists and for other social scientists, as it involves the following understanding :

1. Relations between environment and exploitative or productive technology.
2. Behaviour patterns involved in the exploitative action of a particular area by means of a particular technology.

3. The extent which the behavior patterns entailed in exploiting the environment affect other aspects of culture. (Steward, 1955).

The author wishes to discuss here on the conflict and effects of development projects on the Dange Dhanagars of Radhanagri taluka, Kolhapur district, Southern Maharashtra. It also highlights the importance of sustainable cultural and economic practices of small communities who live in the natures cradle. He visited the spot between 1992 and 2000.

The underlying assumption is that if we protect the indigenous communities and their eco-systems, then their culture and economy will be protected and lead to sustainable development.

Etymology: The term *Dhan* means cattle wealth or must have been derived from the Sanskrit term ***dang*** = forest hills. The dhanagars possess wealth in the form of liestocks - sheep and cows. The term Dhanagar means shepherd. They are basically a pastoral community and are an environment-friendly community who live close to nature.

Thurston, E. in his work 'Castes and Tribes of Madras' states that the term dhanagar has been derived from the word ***dhenu meaning*** cow. (Wikipedia)

Statewise Geographical Distribution: The Dhanagars are spread out in several states such as Andhra Pradesh (Gollas), Karnataka (Kuruba), Kerala (Attiyan), Maharashtra (Dhanagars), Madhya Pradesh (Gavalis), Bihar, Harayana and Himachal Pradesh (Gaddis), Gujerat (Rabari), Rajasthan, U.P. and West Bengal(Pal), Jammu and Kashmir(Pohol), and Orissa (Oraon). According to Enthoven there are 22 endogamous and 108 exogamous of Dhanagars. (Enthoven, 1920)

Dhanagars and their sub-territorial groups: There are 20 economic sub- groups such Ahir (milk men), Dange

Dhanagar (Traditional cultivation and cow herding), Gadari, Dhengar, Gadari Nikhar, Hande Hatkars, Kannade, Khati, Khutekar, Kurmar, Ladshe, Mendhe, Sanagar, Shegar, Telangi, Tellari, Uni Kankan, Varhade, Zade and Zhendhe. Kailash Malhotra(1984:298) estimated their population to be three million spread over 11districts of Maharashtra.

Geographical distribution of Danges [Gavalis]: The people known by above names finds located in between 19 deg and 13 deg northern latitude across 11 districts and 47 tehsils in the states of Maharashtra, Karnataka and Goa. Enthoven noted them being found all over Deccan, Konkan and the Southern Maratha province. (Dandekar, Ajay 1984)

Ecology and geographical distribution: The first known records of pastorals in India dates back to the Neolithic period. The pastoral communities were confined to the semi-arid tracts of precipitation of less than 600 mm of rain annually. The Mendhe Dhanagars graze their sheep in dry, hot and semi-arid and plains of Kolhapur, Sholapur, Belgaum, Bijapur, Dharwad and Mysore districts of Maharashtra and Karnataka.

The sub-territorial group or ecological sub-group namely the Dange Dhanagars inhabit the interior, hilly, high rainfall forest areas of Radhanagri and other Konkan or coastal areas of Maharashtra. Thus, sub-group or jati division has originally taken place through ecological adaptation of man and their domestic animals and through resource partitioning of various geographical areas between themselves. (cf. Gadgil Madhav and K.C. Malhotra, 1994)

Study Area: There were 148 wadis or settlements spread across eight talukas of Kolhapur district, of whom 20 were in Radhanagri. In the northern hills, there were 13 wadis and the remaining seven were in the southern forest hills .On an average, there were 10-20 households in each hamlet/wadi, with 334 households from the total population of 1,712.

Economy: In Pathapanhala and Ramanwadi, the study villages find located in the northern hilly forest area of Radhanagri off some five or six km respectively. In Pathapanala hamlet, there were 25 households but in Ramanwadi, there were 27 households. The hamlets have fertile land and forest area.

The Dange Dhanagars practice slash- and- burn cultivation in contrast to the village peasants living 10 kms away on the eastern side of Radhanagri. They burn two cartload of cowdung cakes in the fields. They also cut the small branches of forest trees which is called as ***kavala todane.*** The branches were then dried in the field during summer and put on fire. The ash so formed finds mixed in the paddy seed plot for enhancing the fertility of the soil and thereby the strength and quality of the paddy seedlings, to be transplanted later in the muddy water filled or fields.

The villagers, on the other hand, grow sugarcane, paddy, banana and vegetables. These farmers use chemical fertilizers and pesticides. The Dange Dhanagars use he-buffaloes and light wooden ploughs suitable for the hilly terrain. They domesticate or buy he-buffaloe at an affordable price of Rs 1,000 to 2,000. In contrast, the villagers use heavier iron ploughs and bullocks, which cost anything between Rs 10, 000 to Rs.20, 000. An example of ecological adaptation. Thus, the food grains and cereals they produce were just sufficient for their living. The social institution of Varungal or exchange and sharing of implements of one another, and draught animals helps them appreciably.

Domestication of Animals: On an average basis, Danges own some five to ten dongri or hilly, local and agile, short cows that can easily climb the hills and graze. They get one to twenty two litres of milk daily for consumption. Milk, provides them sufficient nutrition, making them sturdy and well-built.

Collection of Fruits: They still can collect a wide variety of local seasonal fruits such as jambalam, karavand, raw and ripe mangoes, cashews, jackfruit, banana, and other fruits and medicinal plants despite deforestation.

They also collect *shikkekai* or shampoo fruit and honey ,which fetches some money for buying oil and salt, the family requirements.

Sale of Firewood: The most common secondary source of income for men and women is the collection of firewood from the nearby hilly-forests. They walk a distance of some five to ten km uphills in the morning and bring that to the Radhanagri weekly shandy. A single bundle of firewood fetches them Rs. 30 ~ 50. This is their supportive source of income.

Casual Labour: Appreciable number of people work as wage labourers for about 90 to 180 days in a year. Many of the Danges migrate to the coastal towns nearby for livelihood especially during summer and pre- monsoon.

Farmers Land for Lease: Many families were found to take village farmers land on the assumption that they were strong and hard working. This again supplements their limited income from limited land.

Development Projects and Conflicts: The construction of Radhanagri, Kalambwadi, Dhamod dams and huge clearance and extraction of Bauxite ore from the forest areas of Durgamanwadi village and the construction of roads has brought sea change. These changes while beneficial in some ways to the people in general have proved detrimental to the Dange Dhanagars inhabiting the northern hills near the Indian Aluminium Company extraction sites. The INDAL Company at Durgamanwadi claims to have been used environmentally sound practices of mining, implementing many social welfare and development programmes for them.

However, during interviews of families nearby extraction sites, residents have complained that to be their home and residence for generations and the authorities had cheated them. When reminded about the electricity facility provided by the INDAL Company, the Dange Dhanagar women agreed, but added their houses were yet not registered in their name in the land records. It could be seen that the forest and tree cover had rapidly vanished, impacting them directly on forest-based economy.

More than six river dam projects and the INDAL company had resulted in maximum displacement of Dange Dhanagars and other villagers. Majority of them have been rehabilitated in Kagal, Ichalkaranji, and Kolhapur nearby talukas. However, several hundreds of families have migrated to forests in and around Mundgod, Yellapur, talukas in Uttara Kannada district of Karnataka.

An M.Phil study from Anand J(2002)Economy and Change among the Gavalis of Mundgod, Karnataka indicates the displaced Danges to have chosen leading the same type of forest life in their new settlements, of course, they have now adopted the cultivation of sugarcane and cotton crops.

INDAL company and the river dam projects have brought infrastructural benefits in the form of roads, electricity, bore wells, primary health care and primary education, pipelines, drinking water and adult education. Adequate training in self-employment in the areas such as dairy, sheep rearing in closed fences, mushroom cultivation, preparation of leaf plates and bowls, tailoring and photo lamination, free health check up and installation of medical centre at Durgamanwadi INDAL Centre, village tar roads, supply of 100 smokeless chulas, implementation of child welfare programmes, have cumulatively improved the living standards in piece-meal.

It was observed the programmes were carried more with an attitude of compensating for exploitatation and arrest from the wrath of protests of environmental activists, in anticipation of acceptable image in the public, media and the government agencies.

The author finds two extreme positions of development:

(1) Economic growth or capitalistic path of development accepted by the Indian state and,

(2) The traditional but environmentally sustainable path of development.

Though, it is declared by the United Nations that there was no conflict between development and environment, the Dange Dhangars case study reflected an appropriate combination of the above approaches.

To illustrate this point of development, we can take the case of the displaced Dange Dhanagars of Radhanagri to the Mundgod forest villages. These displaced Dange Dhanagars chose to lead the same type of forest life as they did before. They have maintained their traditional house type, food, religious practices, and domestication of cows and cattle. On the other hand, they have switched over partly to cash crops such as sugarcane.

On the primary education front, utilizing the services of primary health centre, they have shown much progress than their Maharashtra counterparts.

If we look at the frequency (4 to 8 deaths per day) of recent suicides of cash crop cultivators of sugarcane farmers in several districts of Karnataka, especially in the southern districts for June- July 2015, the Dange Dhanagars approach was sustainable in terms of protecting indigenous culture and their forests, land, water and other rich resources.(Vijay Vani, June-July)

Should not the so called developed farmers of Karnataka take lessons from the Dange Dhangar peasants of Mundgod ? They should practice mixed crops and also be free from the urban vices such as drinking, and avoid necessary loans unless very essential. The Government both at the centre and state should have an agricultural policy in which there should be a cropping pattern with a bias towards mixed cropping, fixing minimum support prices for each crop, good market system by removing the middle men, crop insurance, etc are needed urgently.

References

Ambekar, J.B. "Relevance of Cultural-ecological Perspective in Environment and Development Studies" in **Peasants, Environment and Sustainable Development**", Rawat, 2009.

Anand, J. **Economy and Change among the Gavalis of Mundgod**, Unpublished Dissertation, Shivaji University, Kolhapur, 2002.

Dandekar, Ajay "The Warlis and the Dange Dhanagars: The Context of the Commons, data:text/html;charset.

Enthoven, R.E.**Tribes and Castes of Bombay Presidency,** Bombay, 1920.

Gadgil, Madhav and K.C.Malhotra "The Ecological Significance of Caste" in **Social Ecology(ed)**, Ramachandra Guha, Oxford, Delhi, 1994.

Malhotra, K.C "Population Structure among the Dhanagar Caste Cluster of Maharashtra" in J.R. Lucacs (ed) **The People of Asia**, 1984.

Steward, Julian **Theory of Culture Change**, University of Illinois Press, Urbana, 1955.

Vijay Vani **Kannada Daily Newspaper**, June-July, 2015, Hubli.

Wikepedia, **Dhanagar, the free encyclopedia**, data:text/html; charset.

7

Development-induced Displacement of Malappuram Aranadans

— ***Jesurathnam Devarapalli***
Sreejisha V P

The developmental perspective of Indian subcontinent reflects that it has both the black and white pictures of developmental scenario. This is clearly visible in the developmental policies of the indigenous soceieties, who are suffering for such practices. In this context, the Development-Induced Displacement [DID] is a significant issue to deal with. The discussion began in 1960s with different views and perspectives.

According to Chambers' [1969] definition, "resettlemt is characterised by two main features: A movement of population; and an element of planning and control". Displacement is the circumstance, where the people are driven from their ancestral area to another and that normally causes the differences in their socio-cultural life and affects their livelihood. Therefore, displacemnt crop up a negative emotion in the people, where it takes place. on the other hand, we can treat it as a a violation of the fundamental rights of the human beings, as the movement is by 'force'. But, there are certain situations, which are done with the prior request of the people. Thus, we can see different types of movements, which causes the displacement, differently called as the resettlement or the relocation due to reasons such as the construction of projects like the dams, hydropower plants, reservoirs, canals etc. for transportation, urbanisation, industrialisation, protected areas preservation, developmental schemes etc. The current study is under taking an analysis on the end results of the Development Induced Displacement (DID) among the Aranadan of Malappuram district, Kerala. The issue arises with the plantation, construction and population redistribution schemes introduced by the government. A socio-economic issue associated with the interruption factor of the survival strategy of any community especially of indigenous in nature, is being treated.

Anthropological Perspective of Displacement

Anthropological research on development induced displacement was explosive during the 1980s and the 1990s (Guggenheim, 1994, Cerenea, 1991) and recent times (Nayak, 2000; Prasuranam, 1999; Guha 2001; König and Diarra, 2000; Kibreab, 2000; Bhattarai, 2001; Schmidt-Soltau, 2002). As quoted Jaffe, (1962) the term "displaced persons" was coined by Kulischer and applied to all categories of forced mobility in Europe during the Second World War. According to Macmillian English Dictionary - displacement is a situation in which a person is forced to leave his or her own position or space and go somewhere else to live. According to the *Encyclopedia of World Environmental History*, resettlement may be defined as "the process through which populations displaced from their habitat and/or economic activities relocated to another site and reestablish their productive activities, services, and community life".

The internal displacement has been classified by Terminski (2012) into four basic categories such as development- induced displacement, conflict-induced displacement, disaster-induced displacement and environment-induced displacement. The development-induced displacement and conservation induced displacement are of least impotance. The study focus on these displacements affecting the indigenous community. Dwivedi (1998) noted contemporary discourse on DID as being characterised by two perspectives, such as, the 'reformist-managerial' and the 'radical-movementalist. As the report shown by the Taneja (2000) reflects around 21 and 40 million people were being displaced for construction of dams alone in India. But Mahapatra (1999) shows the reports of 25 million people displacement in between 1947 and 1997. The Project Affected People (PAPs) in India account for over a 50 million, as mentioned by Negi (2011).

A draft of United Nations Declaration (United Nations 1992) seeks the states prevent any form of population transfer, which has the aim or effect of violating or undermining rights of indigenous peoples. Article 10 declares the Indigenous people shall not be forcibly removed from their lands or territories. No relocation shall take place without the free and informed consent of the indigenous people on just and fair compensation agreement, where possible, with the option of return. Article 30 discuss that the states obtain such free and informed consent of the indigenous people prior to the approval of any project affecting lands and other resources. This declaration has only hortatory force, but even in draft form has exerted some influence. 'Roles of law in policies concerning displacement' has been discussed by Rangarajan (2006) in the context of indigenous community displacement. He believes them to have their own socio, cultural and economic patterns that has evolved from the existing ecosystems. Therefore, such kinds of displacements are more pitiable than any.

Chatty (1994) discusses a case of petroleum exploitation that led to physical and livelihood displacement among members of the Harasiis tribe, a pastoral nomadic group in Oman. Amnesty International's report (2000) discusses the oil industry and its role in human rights abuses in Sudan, including the forced exclusion of tens of thousands of people from their home. The government troops have reportedly used bombings, helicopter, gunships and mass executions as tools to ensure that people flee from the region. Colchester (2000) provides an overview of the impact of dam projects throughout the world on indigenous populations and ethnic minorities. It highlights the groups make up a disproportionately large percentage of those, whose livelihoods are being adversely affected by development projects – for example, despite constituting only eight percent of India's population, Adivasis (tribal peoples) are estimated to make up 40-50 percent of those displaced by development projects.

This democratic vision of global administrative justice often does not align with the conditions in which these procedural rituals are actually played out (White 1990; Goldman 2005). In this context, it is tempting to interpret what Scudder (1976) describes as the "reintroduction" by the displaced community of elements of its earlier ritual and symbolic life as being rather new forms of expression of identity in the face of a new social environment, in line with the concept of the "invention of tradition" (Hobsbawm, 1983). The manner in which these elements of identity are negotiated had had ramifications for subsequent economic and political relationships.

The socio-occupational view point about the displacement has been discussed by Mathur (1995) in agricultural lands. When the people were displaced from the agricultural land, they are merely supported with financial aid that can support for only a limited period of time, rather the social cost, which is fundamental for agricultural labourers as well as the required agricultural land are absent in that context. It results in the inevitable changes in the traditional activity i.e., the agriculture. The sudden socio-economic disturbance discussed by Biswal (2000) shows the unbearable hardships and the inadequate compensation paid by the government. The unequal distribution of the economic benefits from the displacement as well as the psychological and the social stress of the people while they transfer from their ancestral land is being discussed by Sinha (2006). The 'multi dimensional stress' including the physiological, psychological and socio-cultural stress is elaborately discussed by Scudder (1976). It has been titled in different terms by different authors such as 'nostalgia' by (Zwingman, 1973), 'grieving, by Fried (1963) and 'helplessness' by Murphy (1985). The situation of psychological affects such as anger, hatredness, loss of faith towards social and administrative system started to results in the anti-nationalistic sentiment as referred by Kumar (2013). He had justified with the examples of Maoist movement in Central India, Insurgency Movement in North East India. He argues, dharnas, strikes and protests like Krishak Mukti Morcha Movement in Assam against Subanshiri dams, Narmada Bachao Andolan in Gujarat and Madhya Pradesh are the end results.

Verma (2004) views displacement as a matter of concern because no trauma can be more painful for a family than to get uprooted from a place, where it has lived for generations and to move to any other place where it may be a total stranger. Cernea (2000) had identified the factors of community disarticulation due to displacement as the scattering of kinship groups and informal networks, which are in mutual contact for necessities of sociocultural and economic contexts. The risk factors associated with the displacement are landlessness, joblessness, homelessness, marginalisation, increased morbidity and imortality, food Insecurity, loss of access to common property and services, social disarticulation as discussed by Kumar (2013). He also discussed the exploitation, human rights violation, lack of proper education, inaccessible communication and transport system and an uncertain future.

In the Indian context, there are cases of 'investor - friendly' policies as mentioned by Mathur (2009) in Orissa with the weakness of giving adequate protection to tribal people. This resuted in the bow and arrow tribal attack in defense of ancestral land. On the other hand, the displacemental impact on the livelihood of tribal groups shown by Kabra (2003) explained the conditions to improve or sustain the livelihood of Sahariya tribal group of Madhya Pradesh. He believed the rehabilitation package and general attitude of the agency are the important aspects that helps to remove the negative impact on their livelihood. Hussain (2008) believed the displacement as forced, and involuntary in nature despite such repetition within a democratic system.

From the discussion, social, cultural, economic, political and psychological issues related to DID is apparent. Any violation in respect of human rights as well as the development of anti national protests must be taken into consideration to discuss the displacement issues ahead. An Anthropological study is more relevant in this context. It can deal with the DID on a holistic approach. Therefore, the problem of the study is formulated in such framework, where the DID could deal on a wider perspective.

Statement of the problem

Displacement and resettlement is always in connection with the developmental perception. The development of the inclusive areas necessarily advocate for the displacement of the existing population, without considering, whether it is simple or complex society. Therefore to bring the development of the country, there are chances to destroy the survival strategy of small populations as they are not in the contour of power structure. Hence here we are considering the impact of displacemental resettlement among the Aranadan of Malappuram, a scheduled tribal group resettled from the traditional habitat of Western Ghats due to the forest policies of state government in connection with deforestation and development schemes and being in the context of Maoist entry in the study area. On the contrary, the resettlement brings a number of issues in the social, cultural and economic life and especially management of resources as of a long distance from forest area. Thus the present study focuses on the changing tradition and its impact on the survival strategy of Aranadan in the CPR (Common Pool Resource) management.

Methodology

The blow of displacement in the life and culture of Aranadan have to be analyzed to unwrap all awful ways it resulted among them. Therefore, the present study opted Cernea's (1991) IRR (Impoverishment Risks and Reconstruction) model that highlights the intrinsic risks, which cause impoverishment through forced displacement, as well as the ways to counteract – eliminate or mitigate – such risks. The model identifies the key impoverishment risks and components for the reconstruction of involuntary resettlers livelihoods, as: landlessness, joblessness, homelessness, marginalisation, food insecurity, increased morbidity, loss of access to common property resources, and community disarticulation. The unraviling of spatially and culturally based patterns of self-organisation, social interaction, and reciprocity represents loss of valuable social capital that compounds the loss of both natural and man-made capital (Cernea & McDowell, 2000:363-364).

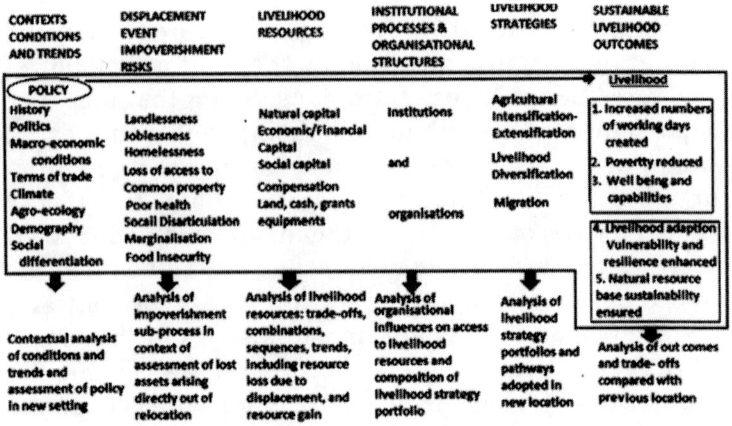

Fig 1: Forced Displacement, Sustainable Livelihoods and Impoverishment Risks – A Revised Framework for Analysis (Cernea 1991)

Above framework (Fig.1) proposing a research methodology examines the risks with particular emphasis on the sustainability of livelihood strategies. The present study undertake the important component factors of Cernea (1991) by reconstructing it under the headings of 'Economic Capital' and 'Social Capital' in resolving the displacemental dilemma, which cause social and economic progress among Aranadan. The data for the present study is being collected through the anthropological methods and techniques using qualitative methods. However, a schedule is canvassed to get emprical particulars on land holdings and livelihood activities. The study is focused on Karulai, Chokkad, Amaranbalam and Valzhikadavu.

Socio-Cultural Background

Traditionally, Aranadan lived in the Western Ghats, which is currently notified as a UNESCO World Heritage Site. It is one of the eight 'hottest hotspots' of biological diversity in the world. *Traditional habitat of Aranadan was in the interior forest ecosystem distributed in the Karulai*

KERALA
Kasargod
Kannur
Wayanad
Kozhikkode
Study Area
Malappuram
Palakkad
Thrissur
Ernakulam
Idukki
Kottayam
INDIA
Alappuzha
Pathanamthitta
Kollam
Thiruvananthapuram

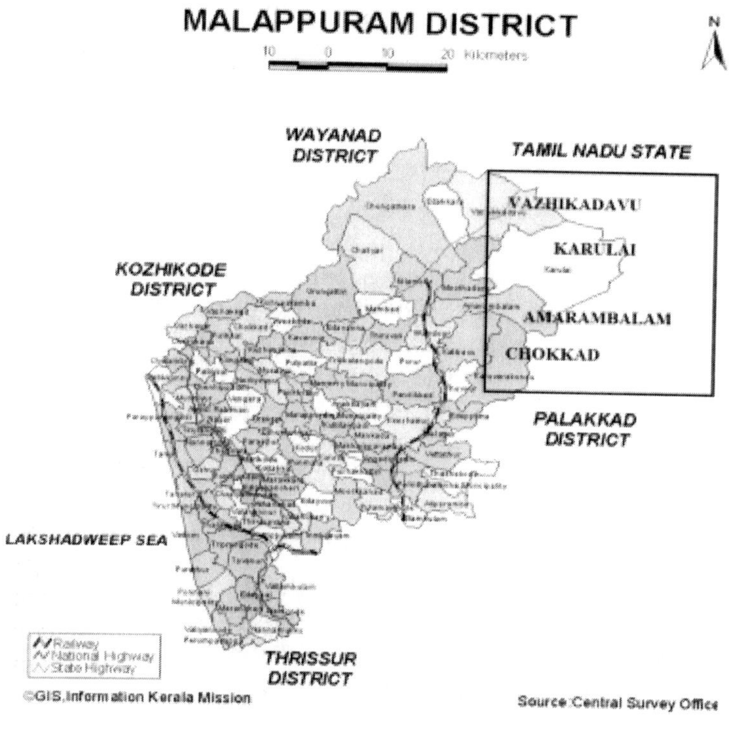
MALAPPURAM DISTRICT
10 0 10 20 Kilometers
N
WAYANAD DISTRICT
TAMIL NADU STATE
VAZHIKADAVU
KARULAI
KOZHIKODE DISTRICT
AMARAMBALAM
CHOKKAD
PALAKKAD DISTRICT
LAKSHADWEEP SEA
Railway
National Highway
State Highway
THRISSUR DISTRICT
©GIS,Information Kerala Mission
Source:Central Survey Office

and Kalikavu forest ranges. These forests with mineral tresure and rich plant and animal biodiversity has been the source of livelihood of Aranadan.

In this period, the Aranadan have full-fledged territorial divisions called *chemmam,* which is currently in fragile situation. A number of *chemmam* was found among them. Its head is called *chemmakaran.* He is the supreme authority in socio-religious and economic matters. He is the person vested with most of the exclusive traditional ecological knowledge. The social organisation of Aranadan was developed upon territorial mechanism to maintain their food gathering practices. Each Aranadan is restricted from collecting resources from other *chemmam* and any misbehavior of his members is punishable. Traditional life ways of Aranadan developed from the rich biodiversity was the basis of their cultural diversity. The material culture of the Aranadan was fully developed on the basis of the natural environment. The *pera* is the temporary shelter. It is constructed with bamboo, leaves and grasses available in their habitat. It is thatched with the leaves of teak owing to its bigger size. They made brooms out of *aana kurunthotti* (Sida retusa). *Thazhuthil* - a mat made out of flattening bamboo is used for sleeping. They used bows and arrows made out of bamboo for hunting. They used rocks for various purposes of digging along with digging stick (usually made from the hard sticks of trees) to unearth roots and tubers. They make fire in the centre of the hut. It protect them from the wild animal attack. Traditional beliefs and customs of Aranadan are being developed on the natural settings they possess. There are no rich customs or practices among the Aranadan.

History of Displacement and Resettlement

The governance policies over the forest areas of tribal groups began with the colonial rule when the Britishers followed the policy of isolation of tribal groups (Bandhu 1986:14). The colonial rule brought out the Indian Forest

Act of 1878 to take over the ownership of vast tracts of forest land, which forced the tribals to move from their traditional land to the outside world. According to this Act, there is a property right over the private forest land that enforces the tribals and villagers who lived in and around the forest areas could no longer have right to use the resources that they had enjoyed since the times of immemorial. Hazra (2002:23) believes that the establishment of absolute state property rights over forests along with the legal separation of customary rights became the primary objectives of the 1878 Act. Towards this end, the classification of forests – into reserved forests, protected forests and village forests – and the procedure for forest settlement in these, were the twin features. The demarcation, an inherent feature of the definition of forests, is based purely on administrative grounds. However, the commercial motive was the guiding principle.

The major criticism arise against the Indian Forest Act of 1878 is denying the communal rights and use of forest. Hazra (2002:19) clearly points out in his approach that "on the other hand, one of the important objectives of the entire exercise was to further the interests of the crown or the one who represented the crown (British), by bringing in momentous changes in the institutional structure and changing or twisting the legal mechanism to achieve. This is typified by the 1865 Act, more pronouncedly in the subsequent 1878 Forest Act, wherein the tribal customs, practices, relations and dependency on forest, thereby their traditional customary rights on the forests, was totally and blatantly neglected".

History of DID

After the independence, the isolated tribal groups were relocated with the Kerala Land Reform Amendment Act (KLRAA 1969), the Kerala Agricultural Worker's Act (KAWA 1974) and other developmental programmes implemented by the government. The land reform bill was initiated in 1957. "Its main features were -the fixing of a ceiling for the extent of holdings, the fixation of maximum rates of fair rent in respect of various classes of land, the surrender of land in excess of the ceiling, compulsory purchase of the rights of the landlord by permanent tenants on payment of a purchase price, rights of tenants to fixity of tenure, and so on." In effect, the Act of 1969 abolished landlordism. It also allowed the agricultural laborer, who were attached to the landlords known as *kudikidappukar* the right to ten cents (¼ cents for 1 acre) of land including the hutments that they lived in. KAWA, on the other hand, legalised regular working hours, minimum wages, and various other welfare measures for agricultural labor (Mannathukkaren 2011:381). In the new habitat most of the Aranadan families have less than five cents of land, which is hardly sufficient for a house and a kitchen garden. Out of the 43 households only seven families have 26-50 cents of land and 14 families have 6-25 cents. These land areas are cultivable and relatively cheap. The changing governance policies and non-voluntary relocation of Aranadan from the ancestral land forced them find alternative patterns to survive. Changing situation along with the acculturation process faster the adaptation to the new habitat. It resulted in the new occupational patterns, along with new developmental schemes, like the housing programmes boosting the resettlement.

The impact of displacement

The sustainability of the indigenous communities depends on the bio-cultural diversity that has developed from the earlier life. In the case of indigenous Aranadan they were facing sustainability issues with displacement. A number of factors affecting their displacement was on during the colonial rule beginning to influence their life and it is now in the drastic stage.

Landlessness, Homelessness and Joblessness

As discussed earlier, the life and culture of Aranadan developed from traditional habitat in the high density of biodiversity reflects on the traditional livelihood patterns of hunting, gathering, fishing etc. The displacement has resulted in the changes of livelihood pattern from natural capital to human and financial capital. Therefore, the issue of landlessness, a component of natural capital, finds crucial to the community like Aranadan as they lived in the vast lands of forests for survival.

Table 7.1: Landholding of Aranadan in the study area

Landholdings	*No. of Aranadan Households*	*Percentage*
Below 5 cent	9	37.5
5-25	6	25.00
26-50	0	0.0
51 Cent-1 Acres	9	37.5
Above 1acre	0	0.0
Total	**24**	**100**

The above table 7.1 shows 62.5 percent have less than 25 cents of land and 37.5 among them have only below five cents. Hence, the displacement is a critical issue in this context as the government has displaced an indigenous community from traditional habitat that provides subsistence livelihood. In this context we must have to identify the factors distressing the agricultural opportunities of Aranadan. The major factor is the unskilled labour in the agricultural field. The TEK (Traditional Ecological Knowledge) of the Aranadan is based on the gathering and foraging, which does not work in the present situation, where their livelihood is completely different from the earlier pattern. More than the knowledge of planting, utilisation of pesticides, irrigation and other matters necessary for the management of agriculture is unknown to them. The study finds that availing land never makes a displaced community to be developed.

Table 7.2: Occupation pattern of Aranadan in the study area

Occupation Type	*Primary*				*Secondary*				*Total*	
	M	*%*	*F*	*%*	*M*	*%*	*F*	*%*	*T*	*%*
NTFP* collection	14	35	-	-	3	7.5	-	-	17	42.5
Wage Labour	6	15	-	-	-	-	-	-	6	15
Wood collection	-	-	3	7.5	-	-	3	7.5	6	15
Tapping	3	7.5	-	-	-	-	-	-	3	7.5
Coconut tree climber	1	2.5	-	-	-	-	-	-	1	2.5
Dispensary sweeper	1	2.5	-	-	-	-	-	-.	1	2.5
Construction work	1	2.5	-	-	-	-	-	-	1	2.5
Teacher	1	2.5	-	-	-	-	-	-	1	2.5
Driver	1	2.5	-	-	-	-	-	-	1	2.5
Animal husbandry	-	-	2	5	-	-	1	2.5	3	7.5
Total	**28**	**70**	**5**	**12.15**	**3**	**7.5**	**4**	**10**	**40**	**100**

M: Male, F: Female, T: Total **Non Timber Forest Product.*

From the above table (7.2), it is clearly visible that the Aranadan, relocated during 1970's and 80's are struggling for survival. The percentage (35 per cent) of NTFP collection in the primary occupation level among the total working population shows that it is still their major occupational pattern. Others work as wage labour (15 per cent), and those in the government sector are 3.03 per cent. It is also noted that some people are doing NTFP as a secondary occupation. The wood collection is the primary occupation (7.5 per cent) of the females especially the single member family whose wood collection is the secondary source of income for females. Animal husbandry is the prime source of income for five percent females and secondary option for 2.5 percent of females among the surveyed population of 89. Therefore, the numbers show the necessity of economic reform policies for them at this stage of extinction with a total population of 284. The above table 7.2, reflects how the vision of agriculture based development perspectives of the government works. It suggests that Aranadan experience of joblessness and landlessness, necessary for agricultural development as the community lack from job skills including education. The government should make them aware of the programmes and policies available on support.

The NTFP products find the influence of international market with the outcome of the impact of globalisation, privatisation, and industrialisation. The increasing benefits must have to be reach these illiterates, unaware of the price change in the products. Therefore, the occupational skills of the Aranadan have to be stimulated according to the present situation. They turn over to financial capital increased day by day. These changes force them to depend more on alternatives than the natural resources. The decreasing importance of natural resources leading to the increasing chances to deforestation. It is important to note that some of them have already left natural capital dependence on the occasion. They don't have the opportunities for wage labour. The rainy days reduce the wage labour opportunities and it is difficult to manage. The Aranadan doesn't have any kind of saving, leaving them to face worst situation. The MGNREGA (Mahatma Gandhi National Rural Employment Guarentee Act) and SHG (Self-Help Group) like 'kudumbasree' is working at the minute level.

The Loss of access

The Aranadan expelled from the utilisation of natural resources, on the policy of new governance and has excluded them from collecting forest produces from ancestral land, where their beliefs, values and customs flourished. This resulted in the deterioration that being reflected in other parts of life such as social and political organisation, religious beliefs and health. At the socio political level, the position of *chemmakkaran* has declined from the economy. It has diminished to individual-oriented or human capital-ended in the destruction of traditional customary rules and regulations. Aranadan livelihood gave importance to women. Hence, the division of labour gave men and women equal status in the society. Unskilled women were drawn back to secondary status in the socio-economic life. TEK has passed to generations through the oral education system as the process of socialisation. In the displaced areas, the socialisation process changed, according to the current situation. It couldn't help in the forest ecosystem to deal with the risks and hazards managed by ancestors. The system could not survive in the displaced habitat, as it was completely different. Therefore, the present social settings provides importance to formal education. TEK is helpful to provide a better understanding of the forest ecosystem. Its destruction results in the elimination of knowledge about ethno-medicine.

Morbidity owes to insecure food

Landlessness and loss of access to CPR results in the practice of new management system with the nationalisation of forest ecosystem. Accordingly in safeguarding the rights of tribes to access the resources ,certain policies and programmes are being implemented. The introduction of *Girijan Co-operative Corporation* (GCC) made them exchange forest products into the wider market, to collect NTFP from the tribes and sell to the outside world. This is a great helping hand to the tribal group, have the worst condition compared to the Particularly Vulnerable Tribal Groups (PVTG) of Kerala in the number of population as well as socioeconomic conditions. This provides a fixed amount of money in return, compared to the business man, who always benefits from the trade. In this context, the entry to the public market paved a way to mainstream life. In short, all the issues force them to depend on the marketisation and consumption culture of the mainstream world. The latter opened a wider scope of food culture to change their sociocultural systems. They have to depend on the market even for simple basic necessities. Moreover, the transport and communication system affected negatively their health and culture. Introduction of mass media as another development indicator affected the new generation in food culture and lifestyle through films and advertisements. The latter shows the mainstream culture and they are gradually absorbing those styles. For example, the food pattern of the Aranadan is rice, and curry, wheras, the new generation finds more interested in the noodles, biscuits and chocolates displayed on the TV screen. The end result is malnutrition, diseases, etc. for the children and youngsters. They find attracted with the dressing style of new generation hero in the films. A new dress code quoting Kakkoth (2004) reveals their health status below average when compared to the general population.

The impact on social capital

The impact of displacement on the social capital of Aranadan is most awful in contrast with other capitals. Aranadan have lost their tradition, customs and practices, as an indigenous race.

The marginalisation phase

Their displacement has resulted in the marginalisation of the fraternity. This is visible in different parts of their life, especially in the social settings, occupational areas etc. The social distresses at inter- and intra community level with the cultural shock must have to be paid attention. With the DID, the emergence of nuclear families has increased with the emergence of individual-oriented human capital. It destroys the traditional social integrity and solidarity. The displacement has expelled them from resource collection to depend on the wage labour. It is only individual-oriented and their social structure *chemmam* division and the role of *chemmakkaran* to have delimited the action for name sake. It gave space to the intervention of modern political system and political parties in their social structure. The traditional cultural practices such as the housing pattern has changed to modern concrete houses which are the outcome of developmental practices of government. They ignore the traditional settlement patterns and the family organization and the emergence of nuclear family. These results weakened social ties between the members of the group and the social affairs become more or less individual-oriented. Hence, the distraction of simple society was amplified. The elderly reminds about the conflict between the community members, especially due to the usage of liquor. Moreover, the present government introduced *oorukoottam* to decide upon the developmental programmes and policies. Mostly, they are considering those who have good knowledge and ability to communicate everybody with and have the minimum educational qualification to deal with the official matters. Thus, the traditional ways of selection of *chemmakkaran* finds affected in the traditional cultural practices of Aranadan-traditional puberty ceremony was completely stopped due to the mainstream influences, poor economic condition and disrupted family life.

Conclusion

The indigenous societies are small in population and territorially-organised. The displacement of such community results in the destruction of social and cultural life. Traditionally, Aranadan lived in the Western Ghats area, currently referred by the UNESCO as the hottest spot of biodiversity. This reflects the natural resources for livelihood, food and culture. In the historical traditional contexts, Aranadan were hunters and gatherers, who survived on natural capital with social capital. They have sustained from the interior areas of Western Ghats, through resource extraction, attributing as their *chemmam*. Each *chemmam* has its own head called *chemmakkaran*. And it is again divided into *villi*, referred to as the family of

Aranadan. Therefore, any of the issues in each *chemmam* was found managed and directed under the guidance of *chemmekkaran.* Aranadan have their own customary rules and practices in connection with the traditional social structure. The unique nature of social divisions and customary rules and regulations were found to have developed from habitat, i.e., the Western Ghats.

The displacement of Aranadan from this habitat with the deforestation and developmental schemes of government yielded in the shift to a new habitat, mostly in colony type, where each household has five cents of land. The risks associated with the displacement of people roving in the dense forest upon hunting and gathering resulted in the stage of cultural shock as well as skill demand issues. A new law and order was imposed in practice of the new habitat. Apart from this, the traditional customary rules wouldn't work in the new habitat, where the tribe mingled with caste groups. They ignore the authority of the traditional headship. Moreover, it was questioned by the new generation who had formal education. The power of headman decreased, yielding to the ruin of social ties between tribal members. This results in the social disarticulation in the community. The displacement lead the Aranadan to lose their access or were banned from collecting resources, but restricted to a few items. The TEK derived from the historical life experiences not in support with the current livelihood issues. In such a situation, a community with the unskilled labour face virtual issues of livelihood. Therefore, the Aranadan necessarily required employment skills, especially during rainy days.

This shows the clear transformation from the natural capital to human capital, which occurred only due to the displacement. Though, the government compensates through different programmes and policies, the benefits accrued from unawareness and illiteracy. From the theoretical view point, the situation should account for the agricultural opportunities. Therefore, the current study ought to advocate for the uplift of agricultural practices for new livelihood strategies with increased number of working days, to reduce poverty and the well-being of the community.

Reference

Bhattarai, A. M., 2001. *Displacement and Rehabilitation in Nepal: Law, Policy and Practice.* New Delhi: Anmol Publications Pvt. Ltd.

Biswal, D N., 2001. *Forced displacement: Illusion and reality.* Delhi: Manak Publications Pvt. Ltd.

Cernea, Michael M., 1991, Involuntary resettlement: Social research, policy and planning, In. *Putting People First: Sociological Variables in Development,* M.M. Cernea (eds), pp.188-216 New York and London: Oxford University Press.

Chambers, R.., 1969. *Settlement schemes in Tropical Africa: A study of organisations and development,* London: Praeger.

Colchester, M., 2000. Dams, Indigenous Peoples and Ethnic Minorities prepared for the World Commission on Dams (WCD).

D. Chatty, M. Colchester., 2002. (eds.), *Conservation and Mobile Indigenous People. Displacement, Forced Settlement and Sustainable Development,* p. 189. Berghahn Books.

Dwivedi R., 1998. Resisting Dams and 'Development': Contemporary significance of the Campaign against the Narmada Projects in India", *European Journal of Development Research,* 10 (2): 135-79.

Fried, M., 1963. Grieving for a Lost Home. The Urban Condition. L. J. Duhl (eds) New York: Basic Books.

Goldman, M., 2005. *Imperial Nature: The World Bank and Struggles for Social Justice in the Age of Globalisation.* Yale University Press, New Haven.

Guggenheim, S. E., 1994. *Involuntary resettlement: An annotated reference bibliography for development research,* Washington, DC: The World Bank.

Guha, A., 2001. *Land acquisition among the cultivators of rural Medinipur, West Bengal: An Anthropological appraisal.* Ph.D. Dissertation. India: Vidyasagar University.

Hobsbawm, E., 1983. Introduction: Inventing Traditions. In. The Invention of Tradition. E. Hobsbawm and T. Ranger (Eds.). Cambridge: Cambridge University Press.

Human Rights Watch 1999. The price of oil. Corporate Responsibility and Human Rights Violations in Nigeria's Oil Producing Communities. United States of America.

Hussain, M., 2008. *Interrogating Development: State, Displacement and Popular Resistance in North East India.* New Delhi, India: Sage. Journal of South Asian Development 5: 184-185.

International Labour Organisation (ILO). 1989. *Convention Concerning Indigenous and Tribal People in Independent Countries.* New York.

Jaffe, A. J., 1962. Notes on the population theory of Eurgene M. Kulischer". In: *The Milbank Memorial Fund Quarterly,* 40(2):187-206.

Kabra, A., 2003. Displacement and Rehabilitation of an Adivasi Settlement: Case of Kuno Wildlife Sanctuary, Madhya Pradesh. *Economic and Political Weekly,* 38 (29):3073-78.

Kibreab, G., 2003. Displacement, Host Governments' Policies, and Constraints on Construction of Sustainable Livelihood, *International Social Science Journal,* 175. Paris, UNESCO: Blackwell.

Konig, D and Teman Diarra., 2000. The Effects of Resettlement on Access to Common Property Resources. *Risks and Reconstruction.* M. Cernea and C. McDowell (eds.), Washington, DC: The World Bank.

Kumar, S., 2013. Forced displacement and its impact on rural society: [Special reference to Ranjeet Sagar] *Vignettes of research.* 1(2): 84-94.

Mahapatra L.K., *Resettlement, Impoverishment and Reconstruction in India: Development for the Deprived,* Vikas Publishing House, New Delhi, 1999.

Mathur, H M., 1995. 'Displacement and Resettlement, Focus on Asian Experience', by Hari Mohan Mathur and Michael M Cernea (eds). Vikas publishing House, New Delhi.

Mathur, H. M., 2009. Investor-friendly development policies: Unsettling consequences for the tribal people of Orissa, *The Asia Pacific Journal of Anthropology* 10(4): 318-28.

Murphy, H. B. M., ed. 1955 *Flight and Resettlement.* Lucerne: Unesco and CJ Bucher.

Nayak, R., 2000. "Risks Associated with Landlessness". *Risks and Reconstruction*. In, ...M. Cernea and C. McDowell (eds.), pp: Washington, DC: The World Bank.

Negi, N S and Sujata Ganguly. 2010. *Development Projects vs. Internally Displaced opulations in India: A Literature Based Appraisal.* Paper presented at the ESF-UniBi-ZiF research conference on 'Environmental Change and Migration: From Vulnerabilities to Capabilities', Bad Salzuflen, Germany, December 5-9.

Parasuraman, S., 1999. *The Development Dilemma. Displacement in India.* The Hague: Institute of Social Studies.

Rangarajan M., Shahabuddin G., 2006. Displacement and Relocation from Protected Areas: Towards a Biological and Historical Synthesis, *Conservation & Society* 4 (3): 359-78.

S. Krech, J.R. McNeill, C. Merchant 2004. (eds.), *Encyclopedia of World Environmental History*, pp. 1046. Routledge.

Schmidt-Soltan, K., 2002. *The Environmental Risks of Conservation-Related Displacements in Central Africa.* Paper prepared for the International Symposium on Multidimensionality of Displacement Risks in Africa. Kyoto, Japan, November 2002.

Scudder, T. 1976 "Social Impacts of Integrated River Basin Development on Local Population." In River Basin Development: Politics and Planning (Proceedings of the United Nations Interregional Seminar on River Basin and Interbasin Development). Edited by IHDE. Budapest: Institute for Hydraulic Documentation and Education.

Taneja, B and Thakkar, Himanshu, 2000. Large Dams and Displacement in India. Cape Town, South Africa: Submission no. SOC166 to the World Commission on Dams http://www.dams.org/kbase/submissions/showsub.php?rec=SOC166

Terminski, B., 2012. Development-induced displacement and human security: a very short introduction. Geneva, Unpublished Research Paper, URN.

United Nations (UN). 1992. *Report of the United Nations Conference on Environment and Development.* New York.

Verma., 2004. Development, Displacement and Resettlement. New Delhi: Rawat Publication.

White, L.E., 1990. Subordination, rhetorical survival skills, and Sunday shoes: Notes on the Hearing of Mrs. *G. Buffalo Law Review* 68:1-58.

Zwingman, C., 1973. The nostalgic phenomenon and its exploitation. In. uprooting and after. C. Zwingman and M. Pfister-Ammende (Eds) New York: Springer-Verlag.

Website referred

http://www.amnesty.org/en/library/info/POL10/001/2000/en

8

Evolution of Traditional theatres of South India

Dr. K.M. Raghava Nambiar

Though the languages of South India are diverse, they could be marked easily as belonging to one and the same family that is Dravidian. Similarly, there are traditional theatre forms spread in the linguistic states of the south which could be identified as belonging to the same origin.

Vithi Natakamu, chindu Yakshagana natakamu, Kuchipudi, Bhagavata Mela Attam of Melattur and Salia mangalam of Tanjavur District of Tamil Nadu (All Telugu), Terukuttu that includes the variations Terkatti Natakam and vatkatti Natakam (Tamil), Kutiyattam, Krishnanattam (Sanskrit) and Kathakali (Malayalam), Yakshagana Baylata of coastal and Malanad districts of Karnataka (with three variations), Mudalapaya Yakshagana Ata, Doddata and Dappinata including Sri Krishna Parijata (all Kannada) and Dashavatari (Marathi) are some of the southern traditional theatres to mention.

A striking feature is that South Indian traditional theatres invariably have their puppetry version asides. Puppetry has two kinds - namely string variety and leather variety. String variety is more prevalent that seems to be an ancient mode. There is a variety of puppetry played by moving the puppets with sticks is also prevalent in Karnataka.

Another common feature of traditional theatre is that their shows are held invariably at night (full night) and in the open air. And this condition gave rise to special style of singing, dancing, costumes and narrative style (dialogue). It is noteworthy that the theatre originated when it ought to be performed in the illumination of torch light. The gorgeousness of the traditional make up and costumes of the theatre loses when the characters brought to daylight or dazzling electric illumination. This is proved by this writer in his experiment of revival and effort to popularized Yakshagana of coastal Karnataka in torch light illumination.

Rice Belt culture

Striking common feature that catches eyes is that many of the traditional theatres, not only in the south but also in North India, belong to rice belt area, (this is pointed out first by noted historian Late M.M.Prabhu of Mangalore)

In coastal Karnataka and Kerala, the traditional theatres had been attached to agriculture. Ancient Malayalam poetry 'Krishigita' (कृषिगीत) connects agriculture with worship in temples. People of different occupations were drawn to agriculture and they became the tenants of temples, when the paddy culture came into vogue.

There is enough scope for thinking that the people belonging to different occupations emulate the traditional theatre as a **cult** that is a way of worship of God. This independent 'theatre cult' might have served them to fulfill their educational, religious and cultural aspirations. The religious aspect of the theatre has boosted their morale in carrying out their day-to-day activities.

The common people used to avow to be a spectator of *Bayalata* played by a troupe, belonging to the temple of their faith as an offering to the Deity. As the aspiration to be attained is major or impossible in normal course, the devotees increase the number of *Atas* [आट - stage play] to witness or even host an *Ata* as an offering to God. The situation is not different even today. This has made a few temples to multiply their theatre troupes to clear the back log of booked Atas (आट). For example, *Durga Parameshvari* Temple *Mandarti* (मंदर्ति), of Udupi District is running five troupes and *Durga Parmeshvari Temple Katilu* (कटीलु) of Mangalore Taluk six troupes to clear the pending Atas booked in years together. *Maranakatte* (मारनकट्टे) *Temple* of Kundapura Taluk (Udupi District) has two troupes. Each of the above mentioned troupes gives full night shows continuously for 180 days in different places of the devotees. More than twenty troupes were in full swing in giving full night performances every day. The season of **Ata** begins in November and winds up in May.

As per the complaint of the artistes that the number of spectators decreasing, some troupe managements have brought about limited hour-shows. The troupes conduct shortened performance beginning from 6 PM to 12AM. This new situation affected the theatre in many ways. It would prove detrimental to the totality and originality of the theatre in the long run.

Cult and Deity

Theatre tradition seems to be a cult which might have been independent of temples. It has a style of functioning resembling the J*hundi* (झुंडि) of *Siddha* cult (i.e., Nath Panth नाथ पन्थ) which is believed to be an offshoot of *Vajrayana* cult of Buddhism. It is S*iddha* people who were believed to have popularized *Ganapathi* cult, also known as 'Ganapathya' (गाणपत्य). In fact, *Ganapathi* is Supreme God of *Yakshagana* as well as other south Indian traditional theatres. The predominant deity of the troupe is *Ganapathi*, irrespective of the presiding Deity of the temple which runs such troupes.

One thing is noteworthy; though the deity of the troupe is *Ganapati*, there is no importance to the enactment of the story of *Ganapati* in the *Ata* performances.

Usual play text would be based on stories from *Ramayana, Mahabharata, Bhagavata, Shivapurana* and such other *Hindu Puranas.* Some theatres of south India play stories of historic heroes.

Once upon a time *Ganapati* was considered to be the deity of *Shudras* (शूद्रा). As time passed, He became the deity of Brahmins too. At the time of Shankaracharya, there was an extremist cult of *Ganapathi* named *'Ganapthya'* (गाणपत्य). *Shankaracharya* took *Ganapati* cult into Hindu fold and made one among six deities he honored as 'protectors'.

In olden days Ganapathi was worshiped in a place, where four roads met. It is called *'Chauka'* (चौक). Interestingly the greenroom of *Yakshagana* troupe in coastal Karnataka has a traditional name *'Chauka'*.

Idols of Hindu deities including *Ganapathi* were *'Yaksha'* (यक्ष)s for Buddhists and Jains, who ruled South India for a long period. Even Acharya Shankara called Lord Shiva as Yakshasvarupa. (यकशस्वरूपाय नमश्शिवाय). Therefore the play being performed with costume and dance was called *'Yakshagana'* by them. The name *Yakshagana* crept into the record in Telugu, Sanskrit and Kannada from time to time.

The usage of Buddhist and Jain nomenclature still continues in respect of the traditional theatre of coastal Karnataka, Mudalapaya Yakshagana (version of old Mysore state) and *Chindu Yakshagana Natakam* (Telugu)

Significance of Name

When we go to the period of Kannada book *'Kavirajamarga'* (कविराजमार्ग between AD 814 and 879) the present day Malayalam language was not yet born. Kannada and Telugu might have been half Tamil as Malayalam and Tamil coexist today. In that work, we came across a theatre mentioned as *'Nalpagarana'* (नालपगरण) which means *'Pagarana'* i.e., *'Prakarana'* of *'Nadu'*. `Prakarana' (प्रकरण) is well-known theatre variety of Sanskrit drama. *Goravara 'Danduchi'* (गोरवर दुंडुचि) is another reference for theatre available in old Kannada. *Dunduchi means* dice. The expression suggests *'Dice play story'* played by Gorava community. Story of Nala (नल) and Pandavas (पांडव) are stories connected with dice.

Bidivareya Birana Kathe' (बीदिवरेय बीरन कथे - A story of hero played on the road side stage or story of a traveller hero) is another old Kannada expression to indicate a theatre.

This has some connection with the modern traditional theatres of South India. *'Bidivareyada Birana Kathe'* has analogy with 'the *Vithi Natakamu'* of Telugu. *'Vithi'* (वीथि) is a word popular in Telugu, which means road. The same thing is *'Bidi'* (बीदि) of Kannada. 'Teru' (तेरुवु) of Tamil again is road.

Nal Pagarana or *Nada Pagarana* is also the same. *Nal= Nadu.* What is the etymology of *Nadu*? *'Nata'* means walk. *(Nata Gatau* नट गतौ *is the* etymology). If you write *'Nata'* in Tamil or Malayalam, they read as *'Nada'* (नड). *Nadu* (नाडु) is derived from this "*Nada* (नड)" only.

It is business caravan referred to as travelers in the above quotations, it seems. Indian subcontinent has a unity even though there is diversity in many aspects. How this unity was brought about? It is through caravans of business people, who travelled from Kashmir to Kanyakumari, and vice-versa. Or these businessmen travelled from Balkh to Cyclone or vice-versa. Business with Rome was lucrative and Indian maritime business was concentrated in the coastal belt of Kerala and Karnataka used to attract business tycoons from the north. Permanent stay of tycoons in the South made way for the interaction between the North and the South.

Sartha and its impact

Carvan of businessmen is denoted by the word 'Sartha' (सार्थ) in Sanskrit. In Kannada it is *'Sara'* (सार). The leader of caravan was called `Sarthavaha' (सार्थवाह). It is *'Dodda Sahukara'* (दोड्ड साहुकार) in Kannada. *Shetty (Shreshthi)*, *Punja* etc, also are to mean the tycoons of caravan.

We have already seen that theatre travelled along these business routes. It is caravan that took theatre along the routes. We have also understood that the word *'Nadu'* is an offshoot of 'movement'. But, later *'Nadu'* became the name for permanent settlement. Thereby, *'Nada Pagarana'* of ancient reference of Kannada theatre *(Nal Pagarana)* established connection with *Sartha*.

There is a proverb in Malayalam- *'Natotumbol Natuvilute otanam'* (नाडोडुंबोल् नडुविलोडे ओडणम्) which means 'when village runs, you shall run in the middle'. Does the village run? Why? How? If you want to understand, you have to understand the way of the movement of a caravan. *Sartha* is nothing, but a moving village - its kernel being all sorts of commodities, all valuables and otherwise. There shall be enough of personnel to maintain the well being and safety of the multitude of commodities and the lords. The service personnel are identified and classified in different cadres which eventually considered as castes. In a later period people of these castes were turned into peasants, when the businessmen became landlords of the place, where they got settled.

Temples were nothing, but the burial places of the lords of the caravans where they were cremated and the deity was that one worshiped by the deceased businessman or the King.

The interaction with the local people by the men of caravan influenced the local language and vice-versa to give rise to a new dialect and the art forms of the travelers influenced the local ones, to develop a 'new shape'.

Thus, *Sartha* of ancient time brought about unity in diversity in India. That is why we see so many analogy among not only in the theatre of South India, but also the North Indian theatre.

The name *Yakshagana* originated at the time of caravans of Buddhist and Jain businessmen and continued even after the Trinity (त्रिमूर्ति) worshippers took over the right of worship of temples during which concept of the deity, and its mythology were reinterpreted to suit to their interest, ideology and cult.

At the time of movement of caravans, the mountain '*Tirumala*' was a summer resort for the business people and they carried the concepts of *'Tirumaleyamman'* or *'Timmappa'* to the south were there seems to have been faith in that Deity all along. We find prayers of that deity in the traditional theatre of entire coastal belt of South India including Kathakali and Yakshagana.

Many aspects of *'Bhutharadhane'* (भूताराधन) of *Tulunadu*, '*Teyyam*' (तेय्यम्) of Malabar and *'Tira'* (तिर) and *'Padayani'* (पडयणि) and such other ritual theatres of south Kerala, have strong indications of the maritime activities of the coastal belt. In many ways the signs of marine business passed on to the designs of costumes of characters of ritual theatres and traditional theatres alike. But now the situation is such that there is every possibility of thinking that designs might have been passed on from rituals to the theatre.

To examine this phenomenon, the costume of *'Todakukkinar'* (तोडकुक्किनार्) of *Kananturu* of Mangalore Taluk may be compared with the *'Kempu Mundasu'* of *Badagutittu*. Formerly '*Mundasu*' (मुंडासु - headgear) of both *Tenku Tittu* and *Badagu Tittu* styles of *Yakshagana* were similar and in around thirties of twentieth century, people of *Tenku Tittu* have made several changes in head gears and other ornaments and costume designs, which wiped out the analogy in many aspects of the styles and the trend of making changes persists even now.

The image design of '*Todakukkinar*' is a sheer representation of a ship, forming the headgear by the design of flags which are essential materials for maritime activity. Many such *Bhutas* are regarded as '*Rajan Daiva*' (राजन् दैव) which is strong evidence that the deity is also the representation of the king or business tycoon who was engaged in maritime business. It also indicates that period of his reign was Buddhist or Jain when there was no difference between the businessmenand the king. The sword, white umbrella, chamara (fan) etc were the signs of a king and these were worn by the 'Daiva' believed to be the spirit (आत्म) of businessman of the bygone era.

Connection with puppetry

Whatever be the influence exerted by the caravan, we have strong evidence to prove that Indian Theatre as a whole is highly indebted to string puppetry. The term '*Sutradhara*' (सूत्रधार) in Sanskrit drama indicates that the theatre originated from the **string puppetry**. *Sutradhara* means string holder.

If we look at *Kathakali* (कथकलि), *the traditional theatre art form* of Kerala, from a distance we find it as an activity of moving puppets. The way of movement of face, hands etc of the characters remind us of a puppet.

Perhaps, *Kathakali* is the theatre form that retains maximum signs of puppetry in it. But the technique of facial expressions they developed to depict human emotions is unparalleled. It is highly astonishing that they could develop such a high degree of communicative capability in a theatre format of puppets world.

When we come to the dance styles of the traditional theatres of South India, amazingly we see connection between puppetry and theatres. The hand and leg movements of characters in the theatre dance are different from the natural limb movements of men. In our natural movement, left hand goes with right leg and right hand goes with left leg, whereas in the theatre dance, right hand goes with right leg and left hand with the left leg. Why is it like this? The solution to this puzzle can be found in watching puppetry. The right hand string and right leg string are tied to right hand stick held by the puppeteer. Similarly, he holds the left stick tied with the strings of left hand and left leg. Therefore, he moves the limbs of left and right sides alternatively to make the puppet dance.

This specialty could be seen in almost all Indian dances because the dance of human being began as an imitation of the puppetry which was, once upon a time, regarded as the main means of worship of God. This status of puppetry still exists in East Asian countries.

The dance of *Mudalapaya Yakshagana* and D*oddata* has retained the features of puppet dance. In coastal Karnataka *Tenku Tittu Yakshagana* has maintained that sign in the dance. But of late, the teachers of *Yakshagana* dance are making mix up by taking elements from *Bharata Natyam* (which is said to be the off shoot of *Sadir*), *Kuchipudi* dance and of course ***Kathakali***. Thereby damage is being made to a tradition of the theatre which sustained its essence at least for the last five hundred years.

The cause of Diversity

A theatre always requires investment of capital. For organizing men and manage materials, money and support of moneyed people are essential. Therefore, the capitalists could exert pressure to make changes in the local art framework.

The theatre came along with *Sartha* involves in a give and take phenomenon, thereby both the arrived and local art forms undergo changes. The art of caravan would not be the same, when it returns to place of origin. Similarly the local form would adopt several aspects from the travelers to change its face for a different look.

Why the local form was different? It had evolved from the stage of tribal culture too. It is the vigor that cannot be taken away by any effort. That means the essence cannot be changed though its outward appearance could be changed.

Even today we can point out many signs of tribal culture existing in the traditional theatres of South India.

References

See '*Divatige*' - K M Raghava Nambiar, published by G.N. Ashoka Vardhana for Athree Book Centre, Mangalore.

See *Dravida Nadu Nudi* - K M Raghava Nambiar, Ankita Pustaka Bangalore.

'*Pandarapuravemba Sara. Alli Vithobenemba Dodda Saukara*' a Kannada poem by Purandara Dasa of 16th century.

N.B. : *Shetty* is one of the surnames of lords of agriculture existing in coastal Karnataka.

This concept is being discussed elaborately in '*Dravida Nadu Nudi*'- K.M.Raghava Nambiar, Ankita Pustaka, Bengaluru.

9

Dr. Mathur on Fisher folk

— Dr. NilanjanKhatua

The author highlights about the contribution of an anthropologist in the field of ethnography of fishing community in their livelihood. Dr. P.R.G. Mathur happened to be that anthropologist from the Anthropological Survey of India. ***The MappilaFisherfolks of Kerala*** is his published version (1978), projecting about the Malabar coasts of Kerala. They were expert fishermen with the expertise in detecting the fish shoal under the changing conditions of the Arabian Sea.

Dr. Mathur commenced his socio-economic investigation among the Mappila [1970] for completing the project work of the Anthropological Survey of India. He made two field trips to a single village i.e., Tanur in Malappuram district, Kerala. The first one lasted between April and July, whereas the subsequent between October and February, [1972], commencing from the year 1970. Dr. Mathur is a tireless field worker and matchless anthropologist so far his contribution and the expertise of tribes and castes of Kerala is concerned. He has widely travelled across the state in various capacities and has drafted a good number of research papers and individual books. It happened to be the pioneering one and finds reproduced with slight modification in the form of new publication in the year 2008 entitled as "**Ecology, Technology and Economy: Continuity and Change among the Fisher folk of Kerala"** from its popularity and urgent research needs for the growth of social anthropology at home.

The aforesaid title is based almost entirely on the book "Mappila Fisher folks of Kerala" and on the report "Ecological and Cultural Heritage of Hindu, Fishing Communities in India" [2008: Rawat Publications and Indira Gandhi Rashtriya Manav Sangrahalaya, Bhopal].

Dr. Mathur spoke about three different groups of fishermen – Hindu, Mappila Muslim and Latin Christian fishermen. "They possess very valuable traditional ecological knowledge of the sea like different species of the fish and their habitat, the various planktons, with the breeding seasons of species. The fisher folks depend upon the Arabian Sea for their livelihood. The fishing technology and economy of the Kerala fisher folks were embedded in and enmeshed with the ecological conditions, their rituals and their cosmological ideas.The Mappila fisherfolks are converts from Hindu fishing communities, particularly from Mukkuvan and Mogeyar. There is no intermarriage between the Mappila fisher folks and the non-fishing Muslims and the Marakkan, a Muslim fishing community of Thiruvanantapuram, who seldom marry with the non-fishing Muslims from thereupon.

The conceptual ssues

Dr. Mathur attempted to describe and analyze the inter-relationship between the habitat, technology, economy, society and culture among the Mappila fisherfolk of Tanur. The general principles underly thereupon the technological, economic and cultural changes that have occurred among the fisher folks since the advent of modern innovations. He propagated that uneven change cannot be explained without delineating from various types of structural relations. He has examined the structural relations in the context of environment, technology, organisation, economy, ritual and super-naturalism in accordance with the functional criterion. The aspects of culture have determined the social behavior of the fisherfolk. He avoided the role of political institutions and familial relations.The most remarkable change in the history of the Mappilas was their paradigm shift from the subsistence fishing group to commercial one.

In Tanur, more than 250 fishing units were distributed in nine hamlets, each having 30-50 units. One hundred units were initially studied in order to understand the organisation of fishing and the share of members. Besides, the one hundred traditional fishing units, 20 modern fishing units with mechanised boats were subjected to intensive study. These fishing units operate under 20 fishermen' cooperative societies. He collected the data through guided conversations and preset interviews, through the draft chapters to a group of informants, made them understand in their own language about the nature of data. It has helped the informants voice about the lacunae and communication gaps in data collection.

It will be insignificant without disclosing the fact that Dr, Mathur was greatly helped by his wife Ms. Rugmani Mathur, not only accompanying through the field work but her help in recasting the book with glossary and bibliography.

The fieldwork tradition

An intensive fieldwork was made by Dr. Mathur in a single fishing village is Tanur, though he has visited some neighbouring villages. The occasional visits to neighbouring fishing villages were undertaken in order to study the social links of Mappilas beyond Tanur". (Mathur, 1978). He almost covered two entirely different seasons – one was the bumper fishing seasons (i.e. October to February) and another - a lean season, for fishing due to heavy rain.The data on technology and economic organisation were collected through interview, genealogies and controlled observation. A reconnoitering tour, for about a month, was undertaken to shotlist the representative Mappila fishing village, as well as to get preliminary information about techniques pursued in fishing by various communities, before taking up Tanur field work.

Ethnic identity

The contribution of Dr. Mathur to the study of ethnic identity is also important as he employed historical approach to the study of the community and tries to explore the nature of fisherfolk in the dynamics of socio-cultural milieu.

Thurston observes "The Mukkuvans work side by side with the Mappilas, both at the fishing ground and in the curing yards and two classes the two classes eat together. Mappilas were allowed to contract alliances with the Mukkuva women and the male children born from such unions, on Friday were handed over to the Mappila community." The Mappila fisherfolk were formerly called as Puislam or neophytes or new converts.

The Mappila fisherfolk are converts from Hindu fishing communities, particularly from Mukkuvan and Mogeyar. Majority of the Mappila fisherfolk of Tanur have retained their original Mukkuvan clan - names, though they do not observe clan exogamy. There is no intermarriage between the Mappila fisherfolk and the non-fishing Muslims and the Marakkan, a Muslim fishing community of Trivandrum, and do not marry with the non-fishing Muslims of Travancore.

The Shafi, one of the four sub-sects of Sunni form the overwhelming majority of the Muslim population of Kerala. The Mappilas of Tanur except a few Wahabis, belong to the Shafi school of Sunni sect of Islam. They are being segmented into three distinct castes like groups, Tannals, Annadikkar and Kadappurattukar. Tannals rank the highest among the Mappilas. They claim that they were the descendants of the Prophet Muhammad, through his daughter Fatima. The Annadikkar possibly converts from high caste like the Namputiri Brahmans and Nayars, rank below the Tannals. Ranking below the Annadikkar were the Mappilas fishermen, who were called the Kadappurattukar, or those who live on the sea coast. The Kadappurattukar were divided into two endogamous groups on the basis of their traditional occupations, the Valakkar and Beppukar or Chundakkar. The Valakkar use nets and boats for fishing. Beppukar are being the hook and line fishermen. Members of these sections marry themselves.

Traditional knowledge

Dr. Mathur's study on the fisherfolk explores the area of anthropological research on traditional knowledge system very critically and unambiguously. The traditional knowledge in the areas of fishing craft, fishing techniques, and categorisation of fish, fishing nets and rituals related to fishing, is explored from the present volume entitled "TheMapilla Fisherfolk of Kerala."

The Mappilas use the term *Baharu* for referring to sea, whereas their Hindu counterparts call it *Kadal.* However, *Kadal* is used by both the communities for referring to fishing ground, as well as the waves. The fishermen of Kerala classify the fishing ground on the basis of the depth of the sea. The fishing ground (*Kadal*) are of five types - Karakadal, Idakadal or Edollamkadal, Padikadal, Vayyakadaland Puramkadal. The fishermen say that a fathom corresponds to one *Maaru* (the length of a man's outstretched arms across his chest horizontally) or *Alam* (depth). The depth of any fishing ground is generally measured by the fishermen with the help of a rope at the end of which a stone is being tied as a sinker. The Mappilas of Tanur held that four *Maarus* is equal to one mile.

Plankton constitutes the natural sources of food for the fish. There are some species of fish that do not live exclusively on plankton, but prey on small fish and other marine creatures. The plankton is being generated abundantly on the Kerala coast during the monsoon, when the swollen rivers discharge their water into the Arabian Sea. The river water contains minerals, nutrients, nitrogenous substances and other materials. Consequently, the monsoon floods help the growth of plankton. Phytoplankton are the floating plants of the sea consisting sea weeds and diatoms and zooplankton are the floating microscopic animals of the sea and countless eggs and larva of fish and marine animals.

The most significant feature of the distribution of the catch is that the Mappila set apart a share for defraying the expenses connected with the fishing rituals. The fishermen spend Rs.10-20 for performing fishing rituals from every good catch. It is being told by the people that it would lead to a breach of custom, for ignoring that ritual.

Fishing Craft

Dr. Mathur (1978) has classified the traditional fishing crafts into two categories, namely, (i) Indigenous on non-mechanised and (ii) Mechanised.

Non-Mechanised crafts are divided into three types

- Catamarans (*Calattadi*)
- The dugout canoes (*Veppu Toni* or *Vallam* and *Odam*or *Vanci*)
- Plank built Boats (*Tonis*) or *Kettuvallam*

Mechanised boats, which are found now-a-days, are of three types

- Outboard small fibre boats

- Trawlers with inboard engines
- *Valiyavallam* with Leyland engine.

Dr Mathur cited that the mechanisation of fishing crafts in Kerala dates back to 1953 when an agreement between the United Nations, the Government of India and Government of Norway was signed. He mentioned that as many as 20 mechanised boats were operated by the Mappila fishermen of Tanur. These boats were issued to the Fishermen's Cooperatives Societies.

Types of Fish

The Mappila fisher folk divide the fish species into three groups (1) *Talepedunna Min* (the fish that live in the bottom of the sea), (2) *Polappu Min* (the fish with habitat near the surface water and appear in shoals), (3) *Idanira Min*(mid water fish). The maximum catch of the fish along the Kerala coast is during the months of October, November and December, whereas the minimum catch in April, May and June. Among the *Talepedunna Min,* the Cemmin (prawns and shrimps) occupies the most important place in the economy of the Mappila fishermen. The Mantal (soles) and Sarvu (shark), Tirandis (Skates and Rays), Etta (cat fish), Kora (jew fish) belong to the *Talepedunna Min* ordemersal fish as per the marine biologist. Two important Polappu Min (Pelagic fish) caught in Tanur were Matti (sardines) and Ayila (mackerel). Kadal Panni(*Edi*), Ayikkora and Nemmin (seers), Akoli (pomfrets), Kanamin (Tunnis), Nettal (white bait), Talayan (ribbon fish), Sura (*Cuda*), Mnannu (anchovies), Camban (horse mackerel), Mullan (silver belly) belong to the pelagic fish or *Polappu Min.* the Idanir Min are caught throughout the year. The Mappilas say that in the month of Tulam, all species of fish live in the Idanir. The fishermen can smell fish oil from the Idanir, when it comes up. The midwater fish were being found in the fishing ground, 20 miles away from coast.

Nets and Fishing techniques

It is important to mention that Dr. Mathur spoke about the nets (used for catching fish) which were of four types viz., gill nets, seine nets, Chinese nets and cast nets. The gill nets, seine nets were used for marine fishing. The Chinese nets were employed for fishing only in the backwaters of Cochin, while those cast nets were found only in riverine fishing.

The gill nets were used to catch different types of fish and locally known by various terms like *Ayilacalavala* (the gill nets for mackerel), *Olukkuvala* (the net for seers, eel and cat fish), *Tirandivala* (the net for skates and rays) *Nettalvala*(the net for white baits), *Baminavala* (net for thread fins) and *Sarvuvala*(gill net for sharks).

The traditional *Ayilacalavala* was made of cotton and has been replaced by the modern *Ayilacalavala* (made of nylon yarn) in the year 1966. The Ayilacalavala is being used for catching the mackerel through two important techniques- drifting techniques (Nittielakkal) and entangling the fish shoal (Valacilakkal). The use of drifting technique depends upon the flow of the wind. The net ought to be cast according to the wind direction, anchoring the boat against the wind. This Nittielakkal technique is only employed at night, because the mackerel couldn't see the net. The Valacilakkal technique is being employed only in day time without wind and current for catching *Ayila* (mackerel). As many as 16 fishing units jointly undertake the expedition by employing this technique with the help of corresponding number of boats. The maximum catch is hauled by employing this technique in the month of April.

The seine net are being larger and heavy gears and equipped with a strong central bag for preventive the fish from escaping and long two wings on either sides, enable the net to encircle the fish in a larger area. The seine net finds classified into three types viz., (1) stake net, (2) beach seine nets and (3) boat seine nets.

One finds some homogeneity in the occupational structure of Mappila fisherfolk. Almost every man in the village is a fisherman. A few of them have taken up to agriculture, though they are not well versed in agricultural operations like ploughing, weeding, transplanting and harvesting.

Observations

- Incidentally, what is most interesting is the fisher folk study of Dr. Mathur has given considerable space to factors of fishing technology and fishing rituals.
- The study avoids any clues, whether household census was carried during the field work.
- He aoiding about the role of political institutions and the interference of politicians among the fisherfolk.
- Dr. Mathur has used various local terms justifying the intensive fieldwork The glossary section is not exhaustive.The scholars, particularly the Malayalee readers ought to crosscheck with the spellings of Malayalam and Arab-Malayalam terms used in the text, through Appendix-B.
- Dr. Surajit Chandra Sinha, Vice-chancellor, Bisvabharati University, Santiniketan, West Bengal has congratulated (while writing the forward of the volume) Dr. Mathur for the voluminous report on the Mappila and their fishing world. He believed the pioneering report will receive proper attention from social scientists, administrators and be a source of inspiration for researcher affiliated to marine and inland fisherfolk.
- Dr. P.K. Misra, while writing the Foreword for the title "*ETE: Continuity and Change among the*

fisherfolks of Kerala-2008" pointed out that "Dr. Mathur's detailed ethnography illustrated how Mappilas economy was embedded in their social and cultural matrix. The observations and conclusions derived by him have become extremely relevant for developing a meaningful discourse on change".

- Dr. Mathur not only collected the empirical data from the fisherfolk of Kerala, but he also tried to give the scientific input with the consultation of marine biologists, regarding the marine environment and oceanography.

Conclusions

The account presented in the volume "The Fisherfolk of Kerala" is an example of a good ethnographic accout in the field of anthropological research. The complete understanding of complex ethnoscience of the Mappilas is not an easy task, unless a dedicated desire stimulates one's effort. The effort not only inspires the young social resercher to take up the study, but stimulates the academicians galore on the the ethical value of research.

References

Mathur, P.R.G.(1977) The Mappila Fisherfolk of Kerala: The study in interrelationship between Habitat, Technology, Economy, Society and Culture. Kerala Historical Society, Trivandrum.

Mathur, P.R.G. (2008) Ecology, Technology and Economy: Continuity and Change among the Fisher folk of Kerala. Rawat publication jointly with Indira Gandhi Rashtriya Manav Sangrahalaya, Bhopal.

10

The Cultural History from Prodding Telugu Proverb

— ***Prof. P. Subbachary***

A widely used Telugu proverb[1] in the daily life of population *"peddala mATa chaddimUTa"* means the word of the elders is replete with past or history. It is used to tell the younger generation to honour and follow the elderly advises, as they came down from centuries. The author finds that as a comment on other proverbs and it may be called meta proverb. The word peddala *mata* directly refers a proverb or an idiom, and *caddimuta* refers olden days about their experience of earlier generations. As such, the proverb comments on other proverbs and says them as elderly words and historically proven facts, suggesting the younger persons to follow them scrupulously. Elders say in other words the proverbs owe to the intangible cultural heritage. "Do not look at them just as our old buildings or tools, but follow them as you worship gods.[2] This paper delineates on how such proverb hides the history of society, still alive in routine usage of Telugu society exposing the cultural history. It looks like a bombshell with wider meaning but when exploded in a context by performing it on other persons.

The author narrates three such events at which he was present and heard the same proverb during performance. He also heard in other contexts earlier in my village, right from his school days and interpret them in different contexts.

Narrative 1: A goldsmith sat in the front room of his house and busy on his choirs on his mini-furnace. All of a sudden, some villager barged in and started scolding him with inexplicable words. The goldsmith had failed to deliver the ornaments to the person on time. A marriage celebration was round the corner in the customer's family but he couldn't get the product on time. He came to the smith many times.Many dates rolled out, but the smith couldn't deliver his product. The desperate party started airing him with filthy invectives.Actually, the smith had sold the gold given by him, to somebody and that could not have been bought again to prepare his product. He thought he could do this on time. This is a kind of irregularity in his practice, which was quite an unfair practice. Generally, goldsmiths have this practice as a regular feature in their profession and make such alibis with adjustments. However, in this case, the smith had failed to get more gold, and hence, he ought to bear the brunt of the villager's anger.

The smith finally convinces the villager, promising to give him the jewellery within 24 hours. He persuaded him that he would visit the nearby town, purchase the ordered jewellery and give it to the party. The frenzied person who had spewed fire was convinced, that made him leave the shop. The goldsmith took a long sigh of relief.

Meanwhile, the wife of the goldsmith rushed into the front room from her kitchen room and went on abusing her spouse for his failure to deliver the order. She told him that when a marriage is round the corner he could not make such gimmicks at the cost of others. She spared no bad word, while scolding her husband. She questioned him: why does he resort to such kind of unfair practices, selling one person's gold to someone else and bringing some persons' gold to some others to earn more money in a greedy manner, and then failing to make adjustments. Why should he bring insult to himself and to the family by resorting to such unfair practices? The husband could not respond or answer and become dumb like any other husbands, when their spouses abuse for their mistakes. The wife did not stop her spree of scolding and continued with new kind of epithets that she was using first time on her husband. The goldsmith pleaded her not to scold him as he was already punished by the party by such invectives. She did not stop. Wedding function is a very sacred one to any family and hence she could not spare her husband. The frustrated husband finally dared to respond and tried to stop her in vain. Finally, he shot a proverb on his wife as "దొంగ పోటు కన్నా లింగ పోటు ఎక్కువైనట్లు" నీ గోలేంటే, వాడికన్నా నువ్వే ఎక్కువ చంపుతున్నావ్ పో లోపలికి.[6] ("*donga pOTu kannA linga pOTu ekkuvainatlu*" ni gOlEnTE vADikanna nuvve ekkuva champtunnav pO lOpaliki"– translation: *"As if the stroke of linga become severely painful than the stroke of the thief- you have become so painful than the customer put to inconvenience"*. By firing this proverb, the husband stopped the fire of his wife. His use of proverb did more than his ordinary sentences had in cooling down his wife.

Narrative 2: A family sat in a posh restaurant in the elite area of Hyderabad. It had earlier migrated from the village for employment of younger generation. The father, an old villager, had joined the group. They had a very nice time and enjoyed very delicious menu. At the end, the bearer brought the bill. The elderly father happened to see the bill. The amount came to Rs. 1,200 . He could not understand about an item therein and asked the bearer what that was and why he had added Rs. 400 at the end. The bearer said it was being the 'VAT' tax. The villager father asked in a high-pitched voice, "Why should I pay a tax for eating?" The bearer answered, "It is the government order Sir and you have to pay the tax on every food item". Meanwhile, the son, who was an employee therein a software company came out from the washroom, heard the verbal duel between his father and the bearer, and tried to convince them to stop. The bearer become silent, but the father forcefully pronounced the proverb ("*donga pOTu kannA* "దొంగ పోటు కన్నా లింగ పోటు ఎక్కువైనట్లుంది ఈ వ్యవహారం అంతా," concluding his argument with the bearer. The son eventually paid the bill, and the family left the restaurant for home.

Narrative 3: There was transplanting on in a paddy field. Many of the labourers were women. Some of them were lactating women, who had to breastfeed infants at home in the adjacent village and return to work. It happened twice to four times that day. The landowner in the same village often frequented to oversee work but had an assistant called jItagADu, who supervised such activity in his absence.

The lactating women approached the owner and got the permission to breastfeed children, but the supervisor obstructed them from going home. One day, there was an altercation, between one woman and the supervisor. He tried to prevent her from going home. The woman insisted him to have got the permission from his boss. But the supervisor said, "I do not know. I will not let you go home." She argued and called him as inhumane. But still, he failed to oblige her. Finally, the woman fired the proverb, ("*donga pOTu kannA linga pOTu ekkuvainatlu*" "దొంగ పోటు కన్నా లింగ పోటు ఎక్కువైనట్టు నీదేందయ్యా ప" Saying this, she scolded at him with her fiery eyes and left home. The supervisor become dumb, kept quiet, and could not answer.

The author has shfited his analysis in each of its contexts. The literal meaning of the proverb is: Donga =

thief, pooTu= striking or piercing act, kanna= more than that, Linga = a two-inch sized small round box wherein a shiv linga is being kept for the purpose of routine worship, Ekkuvaindi = become severe. The meaning of the proverb is :: the stroke of the linga became more painful and severe than the stroke of the thief.

In the first event, the husband silenced his wife by using the proverb, implying: "OK, I have answered the party and made him wait for 24 hours for the jewellery I'd to owe him. He left by obliging my request. Then why should you prod or scold me, again. When the party accepted self for the request, why should you (my wife not an outsider) scold me? Why should you have become a greater enemy than the affected person?" The husband conveyed the meaning by firing this invective. Then the wife became silent. The proverb controlled the irate wife powerfully than her husband's ordinary sentences. Here the proverb conveyed the meaning that the actually the party or the customer has a right and really annoyed to scold me, you are in no way connected to this business and why should you scold me with more invectives than the words used by the affected party. As you are in no way affected by my act, you were not supposed to react, as in the case of the stroke of Linga on the chest. This proverbial saying stopped her, as it hit her inherent ego.

In the second event, the irked and unpleasant father shot this proverb at the bearer of the restaurant not to control or criticize him, but to vent his unpleasant ire for paying huge amount in the name of tax, not for the food they ate. His son and other family members could not stop him from arguing with the bearer. The father pronounced the proverb and walked away. Here, the meaning of the proverb was little different. The payment of tax was more painful than money for the cost of food they ate, though the tax was less than the cost of food. The father's anger cooled only, when he said the proverb for himself. Here, the proverb has a different kind of social function. The tax was around 25 percent of the cost of the bill. But, the elderly felt that paying 25 percent more money is painful than paying the 75 percent of the cost of food. It made him really agonizing as he was a stranger for payment of taxes for food. He felt bad and peeved to pay off the tax for food. He could not digest that, hence he argued with the bearer and finally stopped the argument by the words of his son, however could come to his cool by telling himself the mentioned proverb. He thought that a person who wears a linga should be ready to bear its stroke on the chest at the context. Similarly, a person who left home for outside food or purchase that should be ready for such unpleasant outcome. For him, paying the tax for food is insulting for the bonafide.

The third event has some similarity with the first event. In the first event, the affected person should be more critical of the goldsmith than anyone else, but his wife became angrier and scolded husband though she had nothing with the deal in between. There, the affected person should have scolded him for failure, rather than the Smith's wife. Similarly, in the case of the lactating women in a paddy field, the person affected by the labourers leaving the field is the land owner. However, the supervisor hyperreacted, more than he should as the supervisor. When the owner was liberal and courteous towards the lactating women, the supervisor need not have obstructed them from going to breastfeed children. For that, the woman shot the proverb, conveying him that he had acted beyond his limits. The woman who shot this proverb could not convey the same meaning by her ordinary sentences, for she was only a labourer and the supervisor at the power cannot show her anger, but she can fire a proverb though she was at the receiving end. She was immune for using of the proverb. The social function of the proverb is well served and the supervisor was made speechless.

Now, we have to look at the actual meaning of the proverb and how it got that meaning. There is a narrative behind such proverb. Long long ago, there was an ardent devotee of Shiva in the age of Vira-Shaiva cult. He had lingas on many parts of his body. One bigger rounded box in the size of two inches in length and so, in diameter hanging down his neck by a necklace of *rudrakshas* (natural dry fruit kind of beads). One day, the devotee moved from his village to another, ten miles away. Halfway in between, a thief saw him armed with varieties of silver ware. The thief chased him, in his bid to disrobe. The devotee was scared him to have been beaten by the thief armed with long beam. The devotee ran in dense against the chaser thief. The rudraksha neck lace and the lingabox rubbed in his escapade against his chest. The linga box was quite heavy; it stroke his chest with regular intervals continuously and causing severe pain. The devotee ran to avoid the strokes of the thief, but sufferedd from the strokes of the linga box. In such a situation, he spoke to himself "*donga pOTu kannA linga pOTu ekkuvainatlu*" "దొంగ పోటు కన్నా లింగ పోటు ఎక్కువైంది కదా s" [The stroke of the linga box on my chest become more painful than the expected stroke from the thief behind me, in case I was caught].[3] In the course of time, the sentence became a powerful proverb to comment others under such situation and circumstances.

The internal evidence of the proverb suggests the time of its origin. It might have born in the period of Vira Shaiva movement in the Telugu land. It spoke about the linga. The *lingakaya* (the box of the linga) with its weight, and the ways that hit the chest of the man running in self-defense. Usually, if a devotee of Shiva has to run, he would hold the linga box to keep that from hitting him. However, when the person ran swift, s[he] had to move the hands rhythmically to enable him [her] run. The above devotee had to run swift to avoid the thief catching him [her], and as such, the linga box was striking his[hrt] chest and causre severe pain on the chest. Then s[he] said to self - the stroke of linga box becomes more severe than the expected strokes of the chaser thief. Palkurki Somanna in his books *Basavapurana* and *Panditaradhya Charitra* described the attire and the body decoration by lingas for a Shaiva devotee. He described many stories of *Shiva* devotees and their ardent life.

Obviously, the proverb reveals important ethnographic data of the hoary past. It reveals about the culture of Vira-Shaiva and the ways of their traveling leading to an insecure life exposed to thieves. The proverb captured the history of *Virashaiva bhakti,* the social movement embedding the cultural event,.gives a picture of *Virashaiva* devotee, his religious decoration of body to the present society. As such, the proverbs are being competent enough to hide the history and the culture of the past as they were created in the remote past for anticipated generations. However, the event and resulting proverb are relevant even to persons and events of the present day social contexts. That is the power or the social function of the proverb. A proverb is very popularly defined as "The wit of one and wisdom of many".[4] However, it need not necessarily be a wit that could be "the Ire of one and the wisdom of many". No doubt, it was the wisdom of many. It was also the history of many centuries.

References Cited

MiederWolfgang +Dundes Alan. 1981. *The Wisdom of Many-Essays on Proverb.* London. The University of Wisconsin Press.

Satyanarayana Viswanatha + Kodanda Rami Reddy M+ Yashoda Reddy P. 1969. *Telugu Sametalu.* Hyderabad, Sahitya Akademi.

Somanatha Palkuriki. 1925. *Basava Puranam.* Madrasu. Vavilla Ramaswami Sastruu and Sons.

Notes

1. Telugu proverbs are, theoretically as old as Telugu language. The first serious academic attempt to collect and publish the Telugu proverbs was made in the decade of 1960, by the *Telugu*

Sahitya Akademi. Till then, some cheap books printed the lists of proverbs. The renowned scholars from three regions Viswanatha Satyanarayan, Marupuru Kodanda Rami Reddy, and P. Yashoda Reddy collected around twelve thousand proverbs with wider analytical editorial to such collection narrating how provebs dare express the life of people.

2. The 13th century poet says not to look down upon "Telugu words (proverbs) were like our Vedas" (*Telugu mATalanga valadu Vedamula koladi*)
3. The narrative was told by (Recently, he passed away) Sriramoju, Rajaratnachary of Khammam. He was an ardent Shiva devotee used to wear lingas on various parts of his body and particularly used to wear a rounded linga box on his chest by hanging it with necklace bead . He felt the pain of the striking of linga box on his chest for himself, when he ran under context during his course of life. He also mentioned his father and forefathers used to wear such ling box like him. His father used to pronounce the proverb in various context in routine life. The proverb widely used in the social circles of Shaiva communities, of course, it is being used by other communities, in Southern India. The proverb is functional in Kannada language, as the *Virashaiva* cult was more strong and wider than that in Telugu society.
4. Archer Taylor called it "The wisdom of many and the wit of one".

11

The Tribal Documentation of Eastern Ghats in Andhra Pradesh

— *Rajesh Patniak and*
B V Raviprasad

The methodology of visual and descriptive documentation of the Northern Eastern Ghat tribals of Andhra Pradesh reflects the use of anthropological techniques with advanced ethnographic methods. The aspects of mapping of them spatially form an integral part of the very approach.

It owes to the multimedia approach through frequent contact of tribal communities with the industrial societies and market forces. The original intangible cultural heritage of many traditional groups or communities, as such, is likely to be influenced and at times may be lost forever by way of such acculturation and integration into the dominant sociopolitical and modem societies. This would result in a permanent loss to the unified cultural diversity. It is neither really possible nor ethical to control the forces of change in democratic world order. The loss of "intangible cultural heritage" could result in the reduction of cultural diversity, a loss to the whole humankind. In recognizing this trend, it became necessary to identify, record and document the intangible cultural heritage (ITH) of various communities for the future generations in general and particularly urgent in the case of marginal and tribal communities, as they were more vulnerable of the globalisation processes.

> *The "intangible cultural heritage" means the practices, representations, expressions, knowledge, skills - as well as the instruments, objects, artifacts and cultural spaces associated therewith - that communities, groups and in some cases, individuals recognize as part of their cultural heritage. This intangible cultural heritage, transmitted from generation to generation, is constantly recreated by communities and groups in response to their environment, their interaction with nature and history, and provides them with a sense of identity and continuity, thus promoting respect for cultural diversity and human creativity".*
>
> (UNESCO-Convention for the Safeguarding of Intangible Cultural Heritage, October 2003)

The Development Perspective

We ought to look at the development of international concern. An outline of over three decades old UNESCO's convention on cultural heritage could put us in a clear perspective. The original idea of conserving the cultural heritage (Tangible Heritage) has had a long history of international support. At the General Conference of the United Nations Educational, Scientific and Cultural Organisation's (UNESCO) meeting in Paris (October 17 ~ November 21, 1972), it was noted that the "cultural heritage" and "natural heritage" are increasingly threatened with the destruction not only by the traditional causes but also by changing social and economic conditions, aggravating to the situation. The deterioration or disappearance of any such item constitutes a harmful impoverishment of the heritage of all the nations of the world. Safeguarding this unique and irreplaceable property, to people whatsoever may belong, parts of the cultural or natural heritage were of outstanding interest and therefore need to be preserved as the part of the world heritage of mankind, as a whole. Therefore, it was decided for an international convention on a permanent basis in accordance with modern scientific methods. *Convention Concerning the Protection of the World Cultural and Natural Heritage'* was adopted on November 16, 1972[1].

The convention defined "cultural heritage" as "monuments: architectural works, works of monumental sculpture and painting, elements or structures of an archaeological nature, inscriptions, cave dwellings and combinations of features, which are of outstanding universal value from the point of view of history, art or science; groups of buildings: groups of separate or connected building which, because of their architecture, their homogeneity of place in their landscape, are of outstanding universal value from the point of view of history, art or science; sites which were of outstanding universal value from the historical, aesthetic, ethnological or anthropological point of view". (Article 1). Further, "natural heritage" is defined as that "natural features consisting of physical and biological formations or groups of such formations, which were of outstanding universal value from the aesthetic or scientific point of view; geological and physiographical formation and precisely delineated areas that constitute the habitat of threatened species of animals and plants of outstanding universal value from the point of view of science or conservation; natural beauty". (Article 2). The convention stated that each member country may identify and delineate the different properties situated on its territory as mentioned in Articles 1 and 2. An intergovernmental Committee for the Protection of the Cultural and Natural Heritage of Outstanding Universal Value, called "The World Heritage Committee" was established within the UNESCO, this committee publishes an inventory called "World Heritage

List". A list of properties, which require major operations, where assistance is requested, is called the "List of World Heritage in Danger". A trust fund called "The World Heritage Fund" was formed for financial assistance[2].

The inclusion of 'traditional culture', 'folklore' or oral 'tradition' had been a strong undercurrent since 1970s but due to various reasons, including the terminological and the definitional problems, nothing concrete emerged. The UNESCO [1989], adopted a recommendation on the safeguarding of traditional culture and folklore. A joint Smithsonian-UNESCO conference [1999] found this recommendation to be ill-defined[3]. The UNESCO instituted a programme, Proclamation of Masterpieces of the Oral and Intangible Heritage which highlighted the concept of 'traditions'[4]. Thereafter, it took the initiative and in October 2003 the Convention for the Safeguarding of the *Intangible Cultural Heritage*[5] was adopted at the General Conference of the UNESCO - Paris.

The need for adoption of this convention on "intangible cultural heritage" can be attributed to the recognition by many governments and experts that local, regional, even national traditions were being devalued or endangered[6]. Since the pace of cultural transformation has picked up due to modernisation and onslaught of global mass culture. A question is raised often whether valuable traditions, practices and forms of knowledge will survive the next generation? This has made many scholars and community advocates seeking the means of encouraging contemporary linkages to distinctive cultural past. At the same time, many governments became sensitive to the importance of asserting the value of their national cultures in various forums that reflect international prestige.

The Intangible Cultural Heritage Convention (UNESCO, Paris October 2003) is similar to the 'World Heritage List' and the Japanese Programme for Cultural Preservation. The membernations were supposed to develop inventories of intangible cultural heritage (ICH) and work with the local communities, groups and individuals on various, appropriate means of safeguarding traditions. UNESCO Convention states that the items of ICH must be consistent with Human Rights and safeguarding such traditions envisages research and documentation, education and transmission, appropriate legal protection, and forms of public recognition and supports[7].

The types of intangible heritage that the future convention would serve to safeguard include "oral traditions and expressions, including language as a vehicle of the intangible cultural heritage; the performing arts; social practices, rituals and festive events; knowledge and practices concerning nature and the universe; and traditional craftsmanship." The definitional version of this is detailed by UNESCO as following:-

(a) oral tradition and expressions, including language as a vehicle of the intangible cultural heritage;
(b) performing arts;
(c) social practices, rituals and festive events;
(d) knowledge and practices concerning nature and the universe;
(e) traditional craftmanship.

The Study, Area and Tribal Groups

The tribal area in Visakhapatnam is known as the Agency area, which has 6,298 sq. kms. It begins at the foothills of Eastern Ghats. It has an average altitude of 900 metre with several hill peaks, exceeding 1,200 metre MSL. The area consists of 11 mandals (the three old talukas [tehsils] and being reorganised into smaller administrative units called mandals), namely Munchingput, Pedabayalu, Koyyuru, G. K. Veedhi, Chinthapalli, G. Madugula, Ananthagiri, Araku, Dumbariguda, Hukumpeta and Paderu. These mandals were predominately tribal and fall in the scheduled area. The integrated tribal development agency (I.T.D.A.) with headquarters' in Paderu covers the 11 mandals. The region is being covered by forests, classified as the northernmost deciduous forests, characterised by *Sal* forests, but since this area falls in the transition zone between the northern and southern deciduous forests, the *Sal* and non-*Sal* forests were present. The average annual rainfall was 1,165 mm. The mean temperature varied between 23 and 28 degrees C. and plummets below 23 degrees C during winter. The area is rich in biodiversity, although the forest finds denuded over time for timber and excessive shifting cultivation.

The cultural diversity is rich. It has been recorded that 14 different tribal groups inhabit the area. They were (1) Bagata, (2) Gadaba (3) Konda Kammara (4) Konda Dora (5) Konda Kapu (6) Khond (7) Konda Reddy (8) Kotia (9) KulialMulia (10) Malis (11) Manne Dora (12) Nooka Dora (13) Porja (14) Valmiki. These were scheduled tribes as per the Government Order of 1950. The major population of whom were, (1) Bagata 61, 200 (2) Konda Dora 44, 100 (3) Valmiki 39, 150 (4) Gadaba 34, 200 (5) Konda Kammara 31, 950 (6) Porja 24, 750 (7) Nooka Dora 16, 650. The tribewise figures were being collected from various government offices potraying the Census 1991. The settlement pattern consists of multi-tribal villages. Generally slightly larger villages have at least three to four tribes living in ethnically segregated hamlets.

The Critera

The need for ICH in Eastern Ghats is essential. It oes to the large scale migration of non-tribesmen and development of ecotourism in their habitat. The region is one of vast cultural diversity; exhibiting rich and valuable intangible cultural heritage that ought to be documented. It is also highly vulnerable region, the loss of cultural diversity was rapid and on the increased forces of modernisation. The multi tribal settlements in the Eastern Ghats exhibits local dominance of one tribe over another, while this is traditional, but in recent times, this was being conditioned by external socio-political influences.

We could justify them as:

1. To delineate intangible culture heritage tribe wise in the study area.
2. Identify cultural diversity on the basis of spatial distribution.

Objectives

1.1 Identify the systems of folk knowledge

1.2 To collect myths, tales, rituals, celebrations and festivals

1.3 Understand the traditional craftsmanship

2.1 To map cultural variations on a spatial basis

2.2 To relate variations in traditional knowledge to biodiversity.

2.3 To identify traditional cultural aspects which are considered cognitively as at the verge disappearing.

The Information collected should be photographed and (or) video graphed as per the nature of identified "Intangible Culture".

The study needs to be is based on geographical limits of environmental/cultural area, for example, that of eleven mandals mentioned above for a period of one-year fieldwork, essential to document the seasonal cultural events. The selected geographical area will facilitate the recording and documentation of the intangible cultural heritage of major tribes of the region. Three village settlements could be selected on the basis of their presence in those villages for intensive study. It is essential to develop the cultural map based on the principles geographical information system (GIS) type of database, This mapping could be based on the standard 1:50000 scale topographical maps of the Survey of India and Google satellite images. The cultural aspects would then be mapped and similar studies are carried on in other adjoining areas with a full-sized archival data bank of intangible cultural heritage and cultural diversity.

Methodology

The methodology and the techniques used could form the bases for other studies in future. The traditional anthropological logic of inquiry finds based on inductive research. It was presumed that even if the tribe is the same but due to the large area and wider distribution of each tribe, there could be regional variation in such cultural aspects. The methodological basis could be the well-established qualitative data gathering. In a descriptive ethnographic model, a holistic perspective could be employed, though the concentration would be on an elemental recording of the data. The discussions around documentary photography (both for photography in general and for anthropology) find other parallels in wider debates about anthropology's representation of its own knowledge. This debate has centred, in particular, on anthropological writing, with questions being asked about the techniques and devices used within anthropological texts to produce authoritative accounts of other peoples' cultures. The 'crisis of representation', has brought the theoretical issues of 'writing culture debate,' which has led to the anthropology and anthropologists to seriously question the different styles of representation they have employed[8]. In sum, it has alerted the anthropologists tgaloe on the nature of subjectivity, which can enter into visual documentation[9]. One needs to understand about the issues before using photography as the medium of documentation. There is a recognition that the 'lens' of authorship is as much in evidence in the written anthropological word, as it is in the photographic record, and that texts, just like photographs, are being shaped by discourses of ethnicity, age, gender and class. This understanding is essential for using photography in recording cultural heritage.

Research Techniques

Schedules, case studies, key informants (very essential), in-depth open-ended interviews, focus group discussions would be used proper rapport would be developed to permit videotaping of all the important aspects of intangible cultural heritage. The technique of Visual Anthropology would be used. Videographic recording would be done on the possible cultural events and standard methods of ethnographic filming would be used. The technical developments in visual documentation have become more feasible with the development of video cameras, which were cost-effective and economical to use than motion film cameras. The new digital technology has brought broadcast standard technical quality within the budgetary reach for funding from many institutions. The new cameras weigh very little, can be used in very low light conditions when used in conjunction with proper microphones, they allow a single person working on his own to produce high quality video rushes. Visual images were now much easier and cheaper to manipulate in non-linear edit suites, in the context of CD-ROM devices. The development of hypermedia promises to allow the use of visual images, moving as well as still, in conjunction with texts and graphics. A social anthropologist with sufficient technical knowledge of film-making is key, central to the issue of using visual documentation methods.

References

1. UNESCO, Paris 1972 http://www.Unesco.org/whc/world_he. Htm.
2. See Meskell, Lynn "Transacting UNESCO World Heritage: Gifts and exchanges on a global stage". Social Anthropology. Vol. 23 No. 1 pp. 3-21. 2015.
3. Seitel, P., (editor) 2001. Safeguarding traditional.cultures: A global assessment. Washington, D.C: Smithsonion Center for Folklife and Cultural Heritage.
4. Nas, P. J. M., Masterpieces of Oral and Intangible Culture. Current Anthropology Vol. 43 No. 1 Feb. 2002.

5. UNESCO- Convention for the Safeguarding of the Intangible Cultural Heritage. Paris, 17 October 2003 MISC/2003/CLT/CH/14. http:// www.unesco.org.
6. McLaren, Anne E. "Revitalisation of the folk epics of the Lower Yangzi Delta: an example of China's intangible cultural Heritage" International Journal of Intangible Heritage Vol. 5 pp. 30-43.
7. Kurin, R., "Tangible Progress". http://www.culturalcommons.Org/kurin.htm.
8. Clifford, J. and Marcus, G.G. (eds) (1986) Writing Culture: The Poetics and Politics of Ethnography, Berkley: University of California Press.
9. James, A., Hockey, J. and Dawson, A. (eds) (1997) Introduction: The Roadfrom Sante Fe in A. James, J.Hockey and A.Dawson (eds) After Writing Culture, London: Routledge.

12

Apathy of Goa-migrants in Upper Krishna Project

— Dr. Sadanand B. Sugandhi

Introduction

Every year, dams, highways, ports, urban improvements, mines, pipelines and petrochemical plants, industrial and other development projects displace about 10 mn people across the world. In India alone, involuntary resettlement is estimated to have affected about 50 mn people in the last five decades. The sheer magnitude of numbers involved is mind blogging. Experience shows that most people forced to relocate often end up worse off than before. Three-fourth of those displaced in India over six decades still face an uncertain future.

The history of resettlement is not a happier one. Experience, however, suggests the problems arranging from resettlement were insurmountable. The examples of resettlements are not unknown. The fact is that much can be done to put the project affected people back on the track and soften the impact of their displacement. This however, is possible if those responsible for managing resettlement handle the operations humanely, with full understanding of the issues involved.

The Upper Krishna Project is the biggest resettlement project in India and one of the biggest in the world. The two dams, constructed across the river Krishna near Narayanpur and Alamatti village, have submerged 201 villages and a town Bagalkot. About 400,000 people have displaced and about 80, 000 families were dislocated. Such large displacement has taken place for multi-purpose irrigation and generation of hydro-electricity.

Involuntarily displaced, socially and economically excluded people, most often, in search of food and shelter, were migrating towards cities in India.

Development of irrigation has brought Green revolution in the country. India has achieved self-sufficiency in food. Larger dams were constructed for facilitating irrigation, which displaced millions of people, majority of whom were socially excluded like, Tribes, SCs, and BCs.

Migration of people is not a new phenomenon; it is as old as human history. There were certain causes for human migration, namely, natural calamities, wars, conflicts, poverty and manmade disasters etc. The displacement of people due to developmental projects, mainly irrigation projects affected larger number of people in India and most of the displaced families have been migrated from resettlement colony to cities nearby, sometime outside the state. Michael Cernea writes that development-induced displacement causes more refugees globally than wars and natural disasters (Cernea 1996b: 18).

People live, as if refugees in their own country; those were migrated to other states due to involuntary displacement. We have number of articles about migration duė to poverty, but due to dams and displacement-led migration are rare. How such development projects make people to migrate, even though, displaced families could get house site in resettlement colony and incentives yet, people migrate from resettlement colonies. There is a correlation between the displacement, and migration. Those are migrated due to displacement, majority of people among whom were socially, economically excluded people in India.

On the other hand, 64th round of the National Sample Survey (July 2000 –June 2008) National Sample changes in the migration rates among social groups in during 1999-2000 and 2007-08: The migration rates in 1999-2000 and 2007-08, among the different social groups in rural India display similar pattern. Like the situation observed in 2007-08, in 1999-2000, the migration rate in the rural areas was also lowest among the ST, nearly 20 percent compared to about 24 percent in 2007-08 and it was the highest among 'others', 26 percent as against 28 percent in 2007-08.

It is seen that migration rate was lowest among SC in 1999-2000 (31 per cent) but was lowest among OBC in 2007-08 (33 percent), while it was the highest among 'others', in both periods (35 percent in1999-2000 and 38 percent in 2007-08). In 1999-2000, the migration rate among urban males was lowest for SC (23 per cent), while in 2007-08 it was lowest for OBC (23 per cent).However, for urban males in these two time periods, the migration rate was highest among ST and others (28 percent each in 1999-2000 and 29 percent each in 2007-08).

In the same survey, we can also see the migration percentage due to displacement by development projects. In rural, 4 households, in urban, 15 households and 10 households anywhere in India found migrant households who were displaced by development projects (per 1000 of migrants households), such as, large dams, highways, thermal power stations, etc.

Aim and objectives

Vulnerable people of Indian society, often facing involuntary displacement on to further internal migration.

The migration process and the problems of migrants from involuntary displacement and resettlement remain the objective. Therefore, the study includes some of the objectives to spotlight the problems of people at different stages of mobility; displacement and migration, they were as follows:

1. To understand the socio-economic factors responsible for migration of displaced and resettled people of Upper Krishna Project in Karnataka to Goa.
2. To know the socio-economic background of the migrants, and to analyze the migration before and aftermath of migrants.
3. To ascertain how far the migration has contributed towards the improvement of economic conditions of migrant workers and their families.
4. To study the difficulties and problems faced by the people displaced during migration.
5. To know sociocultural changes among migrants.

A case of Upper Krishna Project in Karnataka has been taken here, as the displacement of people, mainly socially excluded became the migrants in Goa for livelihood.

The justification of title

This kind of study brings new dimensions of understanding about new causes for migration. Displacement is also major contributor for internal migration. It is a double kind of migration in another sense. Displacing from one place to another is somewhat forced migration, and those doing so from resettlement colonies to other places as migrants. The importance of study lies here, because, it perforce to understand the complex nature of double-migration by the same refugees. Here, two dimensions of the problem was carried out; one is the displacement as the internal migration and another about the outstate migration.

The paper entitled *'Displaced Excluded Migrants in Goa'* recast into the "*Apathy of Goa-migrants in Upper Krishna Project*" includes three concepts; displacement, exclusion and migration. We could assimilate about the displacement, socially excluded people for food and shelter migrating to new pasture, where they find work and opportunity. The displaced and socially excluded people of Karnataka lived in Goa as seasonal migrants and some became permanent migrants.

Method of study

Anthropology, as a discipline, came relatively late to the study of migration as a social, political, economic and cultural process. However, by the late 1950s and early 1960s, it became apparent to many anthropologists that migration should receive more systematic attention as a topic for research. The number of ethnographic monographs on those particular migration streams increased significantly during the 1980s and 1990s as migration was established as the central topic in anthropological research. Today, the anthropologists can hardly avoid some consideration of migrants and the migratory process (Carolin Brettell in 2003).

Empirical or field work is the hallmark of anthropology, for any kind of socio-economic research participant observation helps lot to understand the problems of people. Anthropological research is known for its tradition that staying with people and learning their native language. Finally come out with solutions galoe or deeper understanding of their life with peoples' perspective.

Applied anthropologists were engaged with socio economic problems of people. For instance, the impact of deforestation on tribes, displacement of tribal people due to development projects, and the problems of internal migration etc., For the socio-economic development of Scheduled Caste and Scheduled Tribes, anthropologists have been major source for formation of policy.

Migration as problem and development, studied by the anthropologists, throughout the world, to have brought various articles, books in large number. But present study is highlighting the migration, not because of mere poverty; because of involuntary displacement of people.

Dam and displacement of Upper Krishna project affected the people of Karnataka, mainly socially excluded; they were migrated internally and in larger number outside the state. They found Goa state as their next home for earning the work; accordingly, they were working, mainly in construction of buildings on daily wages.

For the study of such migration, anthropological research methods like in-depth interview with openended questionnaire was used for data collection and case study method primarily used to reveal about migration 'before and after'. Anthropology is known for much qualitative than quantitative, and the qualitative method was employed.

Focus group discussion adopted finds the common problems of migrants. The role of key informants is very important in anthropological research. They help researchers to have a greater understanding of the reality about the people and their problems.

The data collected here for analysis had been cross examined, and finally interpreted. The conclusions were brought on the basis of findings and compared for migrants 'before and after relocation'.

Conceptual framework

Michael Cernea's **Risk and reconstructive model** will help to understand the magnitude of displacement and resettlement of people. This model mainly discusses eight major risk factors or sub process associated with the total process of displacement as found in different geographical and cultural space. The eight headings of **R & R model** is as: (1) landlessness (2) joblessness (3) homelessness

(4) marginalisation (5) increased morbidity (6) food insecurity (7) loss of access to restoration of community assets and services 8) social disarticulation to networks and community rebuild.

Much of the earlier literature on migration has been preoccupied with **'development-induced' economic migration** which resulted from unequal development trajectories (McDowell and De Haan, 1997; Kothari, 2002). This supposedly led to one-way population movement from the less endowed areas to well-endowed prosperous areas through the **'push'** created by poverty and a lack of work and the **'pull'** created by better wages in the destination (Lee, 1966). Theories of urban expansion were in agreement with this analysis of migration. Ideas of seasonal and circular labour migration were first articulated in the 1970s (Nelson, 1976; Rao, 1994) and defined as 'characteristically short term, repetitive or cyclical in nature, and adjusted to the annual agricultural cycle'.

Nearly, the studies on the overall, have identified the main drivers of migration as the worsening situation of dry land agriculture created by drought, crop failure and poor terms of trade. More recently, the idea of migration as a **coping** strategy (Davies, 1996) is gaining acceptance. This is migration, somewhat integral to people's coping, survival and livelihood strategies (Rao, 2001; Conroy et al, 2001; Mosse et al, 2002) and not just a response to emergencies.

The New Economics of Labour Migration (NELM) framework of analysis (Taylor, 1991) addresses the multiplicity of factors which underlie the decision to migrate and the possible effects of migration on the migrant origin and the destination economies

The concept of social exclusion addresses a range of economic and non-economic processes and relations to the analysis of migration (Kothari, 2002). It helps us to understand the multitude of ways wherein certain groups of people were excluded based on their caste, age, and gender and were not related to income in a predictable manner (UNDP, 1997).

The definitions and theories of Migration discussed above provided deeper insights about the general trends in migration. The study is up on inter-state migration, from Karnataka to Goa. It projects the poor couldn't migrate, but some time, including the poor and the rich ought to for total reconstruction of life, for the displacement of development projects. Therefore, we discuss about the upper Krishna project and the displacement, to understand the causes for migration of people to outside the state.

Upper Krishna Project

In 1964, Shri Lal Bahadur Shastri, the then premier of India laid the foundation stone of Alamatti dam. In 1986, the first phase of displacement was on when there was second phase of displacement.

Large scale, in1996 about 85,000 families were dislocated and about five lakh of people were displaced. This is the largest displacement in India. About 201 villages plus one town Bagalkot got submerged in the back water of Narayanpur and Alamtti Dam.

In 1986, the state government of Karnataka has brought the "resettlement and rehabilitation policy", under the recommendation of the World Bank, which provided fund for this project.

- Upper Krishna Project under river Krishna basin is a prestigious mega multipurpose project of the state of Karnataka.
- The project is a boon to the drought-prone area of northern Karnataka.
- The project envisaged the utilization of 173 TMC of water under Scheme 'A' of Krishna basin.

About Upper Krishna Project

- The project contemplates providing Irrigation to 6.22 lakh h.a. of command area in the districts of Gulbarga, Bijapur, Raichur and Bagalkot.
- Project components of UKP under Scheme 'A' are as under :

Dams	*Flow Canals*	*Lift Irrigation Schemes*
Almatti Dam Narayanpur Dam	Narayanpur Left Bank Canal Narayanpur Right Bank Canal Shahapur Branch Canal Jawargi Branch Canal Mudbal Branch Canal Indi Branch Canal	Almatti Left Bank Canal Almatti Right Bank Canal Mulwad Lift Canal Rampur Lift Canal Indi Lift Canal

The Background of Goa

Migrants in Goa

Census -2011: Goa's population was 14,57,723 with 7,40,711 males and 7,17,012 females. The sex-ratio (number of females per thousand males) in Goa was 968 in 2011 compared to 961 in 2001. The density of population per sq km in Goa was 394 in 2011 as compared to 364 in 2001. The national figure was 382. The literacy rate of 87.40 percent was far higher than the national rate of 74.04 per cent. 92.81 percent of the male and 81.84 percent of the female population is being literate. Around 2,72,731 of the total population of 14,57,723 were immigrants from around India, who have settled down in Goa.

Out migration and internal migration in Goa

Inter-State In-migrants by last residence

Sl. No.	*Migrants from*	*Persons*	*Males*	*Females*
1.	Karnataka	112, 116	58, 812	53, 304
2.	Maharashtra	58, 750	27, 640	31, 110
3.	Uttar Pradesh	11, 532	8, 080	3, 452

Reasons for Migration

Sl. No.	Duration of residence	Place of last residence	Total migrants	Work employ-ment	Busi-ness	Edu-cation	Marriage	Moved after birth	Moved with household	Others
1.	All duration	International migrants	9,759	1,832	191	165	649	468	3,319	3,135
2.	All duration	Inter-state migrants	228,869	76,765	4,609	1,868	38,118	19,852	60,222	27,435
3.	Less than 1 year	International migrants	1,561	438	21	14	23	08	138	919
4.	Less than 1 year	Inter-state migrants	22,256	11,079	274	356	785	859	6,820	2,083
5.	1-4 years	International migrants	1,973	682	82	64	123	51	520	451
6.	1-4 years	Inter-state migrants	60,771	24,172	1,045	928	6,905	4,082	19,113	4,526
7.	5-9 years	International migrants	1,241	259	27	33	100	40	484	298
8.	5-9 years	Inter-state migrants	37,797	12,700	892	236	6,417	3,673	10,909	2,970
9.	10 years and above	International migrants	4,330	452	61	54	403	306	2,099	955
10.	10 years and above	Inter-state migrants	94,210	28,800	2,398	348	24,007	9,345	21,015	8,297

Source: Goa Census-2001.

Case Study

Case study is an important method in social science and ethnological studies, mainly concentrated on some of the selected cases in the course of field work. Few case studies were described and the analysis was made to understand the detailed and whole situation of displaced and excluded migrants.

Case-1

The family which migrated to Goa (Vasco) from Mugalolli, a village of Bagalkot district falls in Karnataka state. The village totally submerged under the upper Krishna project during 1986-87 and 1996. The head of the family Sri Ramappa described the situation about his family difficulties, while resettling in the transit sheds away from the submerged village. He said "we were very poor at that time and there was no work to earn" "We faced scarcity of food water and everything, we thought further to quit the place and settle elsewhere".

Further Ramappa said, "Then I took a decision to come to Goa, some people also suggested me that I could get work."

Ramappa owned three acre of land but lost that on submergence. The compensation was very low, when he also lost his built-house. The compensation for land and house was given, but he couldn't purchase land for cultivation, which was exorbitantly high.

The Government of Karnataka has a resettlement policy envisaged under the World Bank guidance, but in practice it was not properly followed, most of the project displaced families still struggling hard to get their compensation at international rates.

Ramappa and his family come under the scheduled caste category, an untouchable caste. They were agriculture labourers, working in their field along with others' field as wage labourers. In his family, there were six members among whom the males and females were three each.

Ramappa and his two sons work as labourers in the building construction in Goa, now they are settled in Vasco Goa.

After resettling in Goa as migrant labours, Ramappa and his family struggled hard to get work at the begging. The major hurdle faced by his family was dwelling place, and next was language that is Konkani. Konkani is a state language of Goa; people communicate each other in Konkani. The family of Ramappa learnt Konkani and they speak Konkani now.

Ramappa and his two sons are working in the construction of buildings and they are earning their family to feed them properly. The expenditure of his family is about ten thousand rupees per month.

Social Exclusion

In India, castes are still growing, caste system is a unique characteristic of Indian society. The caste system is hierarchical, stood on the base of purity and pollution. Some of the castes were debarred from mainstream social life, because of work and named them as Chandales, Antyajas, or untouchables, now officially called as Scheduled Caste and Scheduled Tribes.They are totally excluded from social, economical, political and religious life of the Hindu society.

The constitution of India has made certain safeguards to ameliorate with the socially excluded castes, but in vain.

In the case of Ramappa and his family belongs to Scheduled Caste, socio-economic and religious excluded community. Exclusion of SCs/STs from all walks of Hindu society has made them rather depressed and suppressed.

Ramappa and his family members were bonded labours. Their landlords ever permitted them to go out in search of other job or work. The villages in India still maintain the *Jajmani* - a caste-based system, where each caste had a role to play. In the system, SC/STs remained freee-service providing communities, to fetch in return at the end of harvest, some pockets of grains from landlords.

The caste factor in India, is not only social and religious but also at great extent economic. In this system SC/STs were free service providing communities, and in return at the end of the harvest land lords will give some pockets of grains to these communities.

After displacement of the village Mugalolli people in the upper Krishna Irrigation project in Karnataka, the family of Ramappa along with his community members were faced many problems in the temporary resettlement colony. The caste consciousness of the village people were once again segregated according to their caste and dwelling separately in the colony. The old structure of the village again re-established in the commonly residing camp and SC/ST people were excluded from the camp.

At last, Ramappa and his family marched towards Goa to finding the work. The majority of migrant workers settled in Vasco, a city of Goa. Ramappa found a place for living in Vasco along with co-migrant workers, who belong to different castes. Ramappa faced difficulty to get the work at the beginning days nobody among other castes migrant workers helped him to get work, because of castiest mind of other caste migrant workers.

In India, there is a division of labourers. The labours in India are not in one class but they are belonging to different castes for them caste is everything, but not labours as a class. Migrant workers are as construction labours practicing caste hierarchy- higher and lower. Building construction labour/workers have their own network headed by the upper caste people. The discrimination at the work place has become common in India. The marginalized communities are facing discrimination to get work. The labour agents will give work for their caste's workers, rather than SC/ST workers.

Ramappa was telling very sadly that when he was in the village, faced much difficulties and discrimination by the upper caste people, again he has been faced same kind of experience in Goa by the upper caste labours and their contractors. He is also facing discrimination by the local people because he is a migrant. The caste system has made millions of millions people poor and excluded from social, economic, religious and political activities of the Indian society.

Case-2

Laxman [name changed], a tiles worker was a bonded Agriculture labourer in Honnyal village of Bagalkot district, Karnataka State (pseudo name) He lives with wife, two sons and a daughter in Vasco. He works independently as a small scale contractor-cum-labourer in the building construction.

In the year 1996, Honnyal village was submerged in the back water of Alamatti Dam, an Irrigation project called upper Krishna in Karnataka displaced more than 85,000 families. Laxman was living in the joint family he has three brother and two sisters; they were all dwelling in a joint family along with father and mother.

He was a seasonal migrant labourer involved in building and road construction since 1997 in Goa. He settled down at Mangoor Hills, a colony of Karnataka migrants in Vasco. Goa. The caste discrimination has made him get work from agents or contractors against commission. His family and children couldn't get reservation benefits outside home state.

Case-3

Mahadevi, a widow of Honnyal village of Bagalkot district, works in Goa, as labourer with children. She had two daughters and a son. Now, all work in different capacity and earn money. She is worried about the marriages of her daughters. She has been widowed after displacement of their village from malaria, a common health problem of displaced people. They had four acre of land and a house in the village, but lost them in the submergence of back water of Alamatti dam. The full compensation was not received, whatever they have had was in installment, not at a time.

Migrants could not get the privileges of being migrants or settled labourers, their children failed to get the benefits in the educational institution, they were enrolled with, due to Kannada, remaining their mother tongue. Learning Konkani language has kept them insecure in Goa.

Social Exclusion

"The concepts of social exclusion provides a useful frame work that can capture the range of economic and non-economic process which inhabit or allow the movement if people and enables an understanding of the implications if migration in sustaining or overcoming exclusionary process". **(Uma Kothari 2002).**

With the help of the above described three case studies, further analysis has been made here in terms of social exclusion. The above three case studies have revealed the fact that social, economic and religious exclusion have been existed in India. These families belong to Scheduled Castes categories therefore they face social exclusion. They are migrant labourers again to face socio-economic exclusion. When they were in their native villages in Karnataka they had faced all kinds' exclusions and now they are in Goa, here too they face exclusion.

Socio-economic change

In spite of the exclusion and discrimination, the migrants from UKP have settled in Goa. Socio-economic life has been improved and enjoying all modern facilities like Motorcycle, Television, mobile phones etc. Children of these families are going to convent schools and learning in English medium. Young boys and Girls have passed their SSLC exams in English medium. These young generation now speak Kannada, Marathi, Konkani (local Language of Goa) and English. Improvement in economic condition and because of modern education these younger people want to settle in Goa permanently. More than 10 young people ride motorcycle for hire (**Pilots**) and some, drive cars for hire.

Cultural and Religious Change

These migrant families have adopted modern culture of Goa. Young people have adopted dress pattern and hair styles of Goa and tattoo is common in men. Food habit is also changed; fish curry and rice for lunch and dinner and pav bhaji for breakfast, all young generation fallow this pattern along with their traditional food system of Karnataka. Younger people listen modern English music and many young boys and girls learnt rap/disco dance.

These migrant families basically belong to the Hindu religion and castes are existed. Most of the families have adopted Christianity and fallowing the tradition. Even, the young children have been named as if Christian names. Jesu is common name for male and Meri for girl in converted families of migrants of Upper Krishna Project.

Conclusion

Displacement of people may be voluntary or involuntary is a process of mobility from one place to another, that in wider sense called migration. The process of voluntary migration may be internal or out migration is naturally going on. But involuntary migration is also become natural in the modern world, because of the economic development model adopted by the nations. India is developing with the help of developmental projects, which facilitating power, highways, irrigation and drinking water etc. for the people.

Most affected people in India due to displacement are tribes, Scheduled Castes and Backward Communities.

The correlation between displacement and migration has been found by social scientists, Most of the displaced people will migrate from resettlement colony to other places for their livelihood, and it may be short period or permanent.

In due course of migration, there will be socio-economic changes occur. This study has found that there is rapid change among the migrants, in terms of cultural and religious change in other words tangible and intangible cultural traits.

References

1. Caroline B. Brettell., (2003) *Anthropology and Migration: Essays on Transnationalism, Ethnicity and Identity*...Alta Mira Press
2. Cernea, Michael M., (2000) *Risks and Reconstruction*: Experience of Resettlers and Refugees, Washington D.C. :The World Bank
3. Kothari U & Minogue M. (2002) *Development Theory and Practice: Critical Perspectives.* Edited by Kothari, U. and Minogue, M., Basingstoke: Macmillan.
4. Kothari U. (2002) *'Migration and Chronic Poverty'*, Working Paper 16, Manchester: Chronic Poverty Research Centre, Institute for Development Policy and Management, University of Manchester
5. Mc Dowell, C. and De Haan, A. (1997) *'Migration and Sustainable Livelihoods: a Critical Review of the Literature'*, IDS Working Paper 65, Brighton: Institute of Development Studies, University of Sussex.
6. Mosse, D., Gupta, S., Mehta, M., Shah, V., Rees, J. and the KRIBP Project Team (2002) *'Brokered Livelihoods: Debt, Labour Migration and Development in Tribal Western India'*, Journal of Development Studies 38(5): June, pp. 59–87.
7. Nelson, J.M. (1976) *'Sojourners versus New Urbanites: Causes and Consequences of Temporary versus Permanent Cityward Migration in Developing Countries'*, Economic Development and Cultural Change, 24:4, pp. 721–57.

8. Rao, U. (1994) *Palamoor Labour: A Study of Migrant Labour in Mahabubnagar District. Hyderabad:* C.D. Deshmukh Impact Centre, Council for Social Development.
9. Todaro, M.P. (1976) *Internal Migration in Developing Countries,* Geneva: ILO.
10. UNDP (1997) *India: The Road to Human Development,* New Delhi: United Nations Development Program.

13

'Quilt' as the Folk-Art

— *Shobha Shivaprasad Nayak*

Abstract

The contemporary collage and Batik arts are inspired by the age old Quilt Art. In folk-art, we can study quilt art present across the country besides in Karnataka. The Government of India has not been able to recognise this art and support by means of any finance or technical expertise to cultivate the quilt art or quilt workers.

Key words: *Quilt, Folk, Art.*

Scriptures claim the art to have the history of more than 100 years. Odd old scriptures tell us depicting the useage of the art in the ancient times found tell that this art has the history of more than 100 years. Good old scriptures tell us depicting the usage of this art in the ancient times. "*Charak Samhita*" of second century B.C. claims the quilt as "*Kantha*". Quilt is mentioned in Sarvajna' Proverbs [vachanas]. It is known as *Koudi* in Kannada, *Kavandi* in Tamil, *Kaviyan* in Malayalam, *Kantha* in Hindi, *Vaakal* in Marathi. In Dictionaries, it is defined as Quilt *noun* 1. A warm bed covering made of padding enclosed between layers of fabrics. 2. A bed spread with decorative stiching –origin old French 'cuilte'. *Adjective* made of two layers of fabric with padding in between them.

There is no age bar for quilt making. Women start making quilts. Gossip makers do repeat the exercise, some as hobbies, while others for the liveihood. In northern Karnataka region of Belgaum leaving '*Mannettina Amavase* (special festival on moonless night) rest of the days they make quilt. There is a community called as '*Gondaligas*' they make quilts and sell it. This community ladies are more in Hebballi, Dharwad District, North Karnataka region.

Materials for making Quilts

(a) Old/worne out clothes and colourful pieces of cloth – old/worne out clothes are major requirement for making quilt. They make design on quilts, by colourful pieces of clothes.

(b) *Kudogolu* (scissors) – The old generation people use *kudogolu* to cut the clothes, but now the pair of scissors are being used to cut the clothes.

(c) Needle – small and big size needles are being used to make quilts. The small needles are being used to design, while the main stitches are being done by big needles. The needle is poked into the quilt until the quilt finds completed. People make the quilts whenever they find time. They believe giving needles to neighbours befoer completing the quilt would bring misfortune.

(d) Thread – The threads in earlier days were made using cotton, but now the quilt makers get readymade threads from shops. Usually, the white colour threads are used to make quilts. Colourful threads are not very often used .

(e) Quilt making season – Quilts usually are not made in winter, because the clothes find dampened due to moisture absorption. The needle does not penetrate into it. The summer season is good for their making. Old clothes were collected and washed thoroughly so that won't affect while making quilts.

Quilt making methods

'Lavi'

The beginning of the quilt making women wash a large cloth and spread it on the corridor of the house. They put small pieces of clothes and stitch them together. For this they call 'Lavi'. This is done on *Ugadi* or some auspicious day. There is a belief that it should start on Wednesday or Saturday or else *Dhanista Nakshatra panchak* hora. Three four women sit together and make the base of the quilt using saris or dhotis. They keep 3-4 folds of clothes and stitch between six inch-gap. After 'Lavi', they keep it in sun. They worship (puja-punaskar) and start the next step of making the quilt, when it is dried. If they start stitching from one corner, they should not leave it until they reach the same corner. There is also a belief that if a cat passes in front of the quilt, the stitches are removed back. The day they have started weaving, the first complete round should be finished on the same day. Keeping the quilt aside, calls for securing its eight-fold with a stone weight. The dried quilt helps stitching without much ado.

Lastly, they cut colourful clothes and patch on the quilts, so that the product looks very attractive. Even sari borders are stitched to the corners of quilts, to make them very attractive and decorative. In 15-20 days, the quilt will be stitched. Women express their feelings and emotions through such designs. The designs are not only a message, but also it shows the talent of rural women. Worne out clothes make a beautiful new quilt. The dexterity and creativity of women reflects their aesthetic appeal.

The professional quilt makers go to collect clothes from others or while giving back quilt they are respected traditionally by the people. They respect them by making them sit down and gift pulses, serials, money and new clothes. The price increases for the quilt with respect to the pictures and designs created on the quilt. Some provide the requirements to make the quilt and pay only for weaving charges. In olden days, they use to give serials, pulses, clothes with these they would also give money known as '*chaaz*'. In folklores, they ask money as per the choice of givers. It is called as '*Khushi*'. For love, respect and emotions was given more importance. Quilt makers were treated as the base of the society.

Types of quilt

In Northern Karnataka there are two types of quilts.

1. *Doddavar Koudi*:

   Doddavara Koudi finds use for all, mainly elders. This mostly measures 7x5 sq ft. Every year new quilts are made at home. To make it easier for wash the length of the quilt is reduced to 5x5 sq ft.

2. *Tottila Koudi*

   Tottilkoudi is meant to use in the cradle for small kids. Before the child is born the grandmother makes quilt for her grand children or gives it to the quilt makers to weave it for her grandchild.

When the child is born and its going to his father's house, the grandmother gives Doddavara koudi to child's mother; and Tottila koudi to her grandchild. This tradition is being followed even now in some parts of northern Karnataka. Tottila koudi is more innovative with designs and colours. As the child grew, the pictures were being observed by that when s[he] tries to inculcate into him [her].While using the quilt, it is believed that outer part is not touching the body; if so then you will have bad dreams and good things seldom happen.

Quilt Designs

Day-to-day experiences were the main sources for the designs of quilts. The characters and scenes of the myths, historical places, persons, symbols of religions, social beliefs and nature were also the main source of designs. In northern Karnataka region quilts, commonly we find the pictures of Rama's cradle, Luv-Kush, Ram-Lakshman-Sita, Maya Mruga, Ashwa, Hanuman, Abhimanyu' chakra, Radha-Krishna, Pandavas, Dharma Rays's feet. Hampi, Gokarna, Tirupati etc, the visited historical places, they weave the designs of temples, pallakki and etc in the specimens.

Each person believes his religion and caste so that devotion (Bhakti) find reflected on his quilts. They make designs of Linga, Iswar, Swastika, Tirthankar, Shubh-Labh, Om etc. Festivals and marriages scenes were also seen on them. These show the social beliefs and traditions of the people.The corners of the quilt were well decorated with colourful clothes. The stitches all together come and join at the centre making that more geometrical in appearance, which gives a rich aesthetic look.

An educated person coul express his emotions, expressions through words, but an illiterate on his feelings or regionality through clothes, language, food habits and mainly art. The regionality of the person knowingly or unknowingly, is put into his art. So, by this specific art or regionality is being introduced. The same way quilt represents the northern Karnataka's tradition. Quilt is used all over the world, but varies from the region to region by its designs. In northern Karnataka, quilt is also worshiped. For example, In Hubli, *Siddharuda Swami*'s quilt is still worshiped after him, the sage was a very simple man, who used the quilt in his day-to-day life. After his death in order to pay respects, the folloers worship his quilt even today.

Specialities of Quilt

1. Quilt remains cool in summer and turns warm in winter season.

2. Quilt can be used for almost 5-8-10 yrs.
3. Healthwise, the quilts are good for use. In rural areas, they call it as the poor man's winter rug.
4. Quilt is made best out of waste material.
5. Quilt is a folk art and represents a particular region.
6. It is astonishing to find the recycling in the way back.

Conclusion

Quilt is a kind of folk art. In ancient time, it took place in every house and heart of human being. The folk-art has their own attraction and identity, because they were born amongst the community. They have become part and parcel of their day-to-day livelyhood. Like other relations, there is a bonding developed between the quilt and the user-person. The usage of quilt in their day-to-day life worne out and softens itself. Still, the people who use do not wish to throw it. In the later years, it comes to the usage as the children's mattress and continue to become their linkage. At one juncture, this becomes useless. It is decided to burn and the left over ashes mixed in the oil could be used to paint the bamboo baskets and other kitchen articles, by drying them for further usage so that their life span could be extended.

For collage and batik arts, the quilt has been the foundation. For collage, coloured and cut papers were designed and sticked, so also in batik, wax colours were used to colour the pictures on the clothes. Unlike quilt art in collage art, different shapes and designs were used for the attractive looks, same way through quilt, which was also one of the folk art, seen all over India, northern Karnataka represents and dominates together with the local traditions and upholding of the rich culture.

Changes came about as progress in technology and life style. The quilts gradually started disappearing from our life. Quilt weavers have been deprived of any means of government support; neither in the form of finance, nor their promotion nor the support. Hence, if the government takes necessary steps to identify this rich art for support and promotion, the effort could be glorified so that modern world assimilate with the mosaic art without going extinct.

References

Janapada Sahitya Darshana-7, Ed by: Dr. S.M. Vrushabhendra-swami, Pub by: Institute of Kannada studies, Karnataka University, Dharwad, Karnataka, March 1982.

Karnataka Janapada, Ed by: Dr.G.S.Shivarudrappa, Pub by: Prasaranga Bangalore University, Bangalore, Karnataka 1981.

Karnataka Janapada Kalegalu, Ed by: Sri. Go.Ru.Chennabasappa Pub by:*Kannada Sahitya Parishat*, Bangalore, Karnataka 1977.

Quilt makers were interviewed for data collection.

14

Women in Folklore: A Study of "Makkappothi Theyyam" in North Malabar

*— Shruthi T.V**

Abstract

Expressive tradition is one of the concrete manifestations of social structure. Folklore, an expressive tradition of ordinary people and a part of their culture plays an important role in transmitting culture and preserving tradition. This is more symbolic in its expressions of social structure and normative values. In this context, the author analyses the myth of the Theyyam Kadangode Makkam, *in an Anthropological perspective. The myth is expressive of the family structure, status of women, customs and traditions based on gender and caste, values of purity and pollution in a society where matriliny prevailed. How the intangible cultural heritage of folklore and the norms have symbolised in its performative manifestations, changing social norms on their status, were evoked in this myth of* Kadangode Makkam.

Introduction

Kerala has a rich variety of folk arts, under the ritualistic activities of different religious groups. Folk tales, festivities, beliefs, songs, and dances etc., drew their themes from mythology and agricultural activities besides the real incidents in life. It throws light on the cultural heritage and social life of the people. The ceremonial and ritualistic institutions are being supported by folk literature, while worshipping gods - goddesses. The themes in each society are being culturally defined on specific functions.

The folklore of *Kolathu Nadu*[1] is connected with religious and spiritual needs. The ritual dances are being staged in temples to propitiate the diety. *Theyyam* is one such ritual form of worship in northern Kerala. It is the dance of God. *Theyyam* is the corrupted word of *Daivam,* which means God. The performer is often believed to be the impersonator of the popular deity. The expressive feature of *theyyam* is rhythmic dances. The performer gets possessed and gives the expression to those activities of the diety till he gives up the role. This performing art is the traditional occupation of particular caste called *Malayan, Vannan, Velan, Pulayan, Munnuttan* etc.[2]

Myths related to mother goddesses indicate the woman, who challenge the prevalent customs and traditions of patriarchy to become the victims, evolved as the goddesses. The importance of folklore for the study about the life and the status of women is understood far away from books.

According to Malinowski, "myth expresses, enhances and codifies beliefs; it safeguards and enforces the morality; it vouches for the efficiency of the ritual and contains the practical rules for guidance of the mass. Myth is thus a vital ingredient of human civilisation; it is not an idle tale, but hard worked active force; it is not an intellectual explanation or an artistic imagery, but a pragmatic charter of primitive faith and moral wisdom"[3].

Levi Strauss also believes that myths of primitive people reveal a kind of truth about the nature and working of human mind. "One of the many conclusions of an Anthropological research, notwithstanding, the cultural differences between the several parts of mankind, the human mind is everywhere one and the same; and has similar capacities. In the mythology, the world over, we have deities or the supernatural elements, which play the intermediary roles in between the power above and the humanity below."[4].

Emile Durkheim has analysed the social functions of of the ritual to be, the disciplinary and preparatory function, the cohesive function, the revitalising function and the euphoric function. The vigorous singing accompanying such worship and ceremonies could see how effective it was in producing an atmosphere, wherein the importance of symbolic performances becomes comprehensible.

The work of Indra Deva[5] gave a complete review on the oral literature of a large region of northern India through the analysis of the content of Bhojpuri folk songs. J.J Pallath[6] presented an analytical study on *Theyyam* besides the integral relation that exists between ethno-folk performance and their basic personality. Dan Ben Amos[7] explores the theoretical implications for such analysis and interpretation of folklore. Mazharul Islam[8] critically examines about the function of folklore, as the pulse of the people. Nandini Sahu[9] analyses how the literature represents on the real life of women.

Makkappothi - The Goddess of fertility

The cult of the goddess of fertility, *Makkappothi*[10] consists of pluralistic manifestations that are religious and social - in nature. '*Makkavum makkalum*'[11] is a *theyyam* performing in Kannur district, northern Kerala. The myths behind this cult were indicative of changing social norms on women's status. Mother goddesses are being worshipped for different purposes like acquisition of knowledge, courage, health, and fertility. Their myth exposes the women becoming the victims of customs and the traditions of patriarchy, as goddesses. The cruelty of brothers due to the role played by their wives from the jealousies and rivalries leads to the death of *Makkam* and her kids. The motherhood is being interpreted as the ground for jealousy. *Makkam,* as such finds being worshipped as the deity of fertility by the folk.

The myth

Makkam was the lone girl child of thirteen children of *Unnichira* couple of *Kadangode*[12] family in *Kunhimangalam.* She was educated and married later to one of her relatives. The couple begets two children and were living happily. Her frustrated sisters-in-law have no children became jealous of her being loved by her brothers. The latter wait for a chance to discredit her in the eyes of brothers. They fabricate an episode of her linking *Makkam* with a *Vaniya*[13] youth, who came to the house with oil as an offering to the family diety of *Kadangode* when her brothers reach the battle front.

The brothers on their returning victorious from a battle, decide to kill her for bringing the family into ignominy. The latter took her with children on a long trip, in the pretext of, showing her a *divine lamp, deep inside a well.* She fails to foresee the treachery and the fate awaiting her, but follows them. After the long trek, when the kids felt hungry and thirsty, she went into a house- *Chala Puthiya Veetil.* The house owner gave enough milk for the children. *Makkam* removed her ornaments and entrusted them with the host and moved ahead with her journey. The brothers, eventually showed her a well, and told to peep into trace the *divine lamp.* They beheaded her and dumped the bodies of her children into the well.

The brothers went on fighting with each other and died on the spot after a few days. The *Kadangode house* caught fire and was destroyed except a few divine spots and materials. The sisters-in-law also died in the fire. The

Kadangode family members started perfoming the *theyyyam* of *Makkam* and her kids, as per astrological calculation. The family members of the house of *Chala Puthiya Veetil* began to feel certain divine happenings in the house. The performance of *theyyam* of *Makkam* and her kids was the outcome.

Analysis

In a matrilineal family, girl child is necessary for the family endorsing its significance. It involves the inheritance of succession through sister's children. The eldest male member was vested with the power of managing the joint property despite its status. The analysis of the content of folklore expresses about the intimate aspect of family relation, status and anxieties of woman, intercaste attitudes etc. The joint family not only shows here the pattern of cooperation, but those tensions and conflicts, especially of woman. The relation between brother and sister finds pictured as extremely affectionate. The female inheritance and the authority exercised by mother's brother explain the reasons for brother-sister relation in the matrilineal descent.

Though, the descent finds traced through female line, males such as brothers or maternal uncle holds the authority of the group, leading to the oppression of woman with respect and support between the siblings. Their mutual obligation towards one another exists from birth. Two or more brother's pattern, where they move for adventure together is a very important feature of the Indian society. The patterns play a role in the tradition of joint inheritance and their management of the family property.

Women's barrenness is considered to be the greatest misfortune in any society. Motherhood is being regarded as the supreme function of woman. Women appear to be more inclined to perform their social obligation, as a sister, wife and mother. Their activities are being confined within the boundaries of four walls. The jealousies and rivalries of sisters-in-law, owe to the frustration faced in husband's residence. The cruelty of brothers due to the role play of wives leads to the death of *Makkam* and her kids. Her motherhood is the reason. *Makkam,* as such, finds glorified, as the deity of fertility, where the brothers and their wives have died, by her curse, justified about the myth, as a moral value to the society.

A woman's ambitious style of living, performance of religious rituals with customs and dependence on man find reflected in the myth. The cultural values, the work patterns, the roles of men and women in the society resonate accordingly. The kinship terms and their obligations, the institutions of family and marriage, the inheritance of property follow the nature of diverse relationship in the joint family, with built-in tensions, and the resentment of woman etc. exposing the basis for the misfortune of *Makkam.* The family influences the whole life of the society. The changes reverberate through the whole social structure. This is a transitional picture of the initial decay of joint family system. The process of social change emerges as a powerful phenomenon, making the folklore to have a closer link with that process.

The attitudes of different castes toward each other, including that of the lower caste towards higher, customs and traditions were based on the gender, the caste, the values of purity and pollution etc. in the society. The Hindu caste system finds testified within a few days of endogamous, hierarchically ranked social group associated with a particular traditional occupation and cooperation between the castes, in terms of service. This type of social structure gives a chance to the sisters-in-law of *Makkam* to deceive her. This indicates a critique of the traditions and customs, which have evil effects on the life of women.

Conclusion

Deities are the creations of mind. Their existence depends on faith. Women used this spiritual act as a strategy against oppression and violence by patriarchy. Things that cannot be done in physical world find satisfied by attaining spiritual power. Thinking and the feeling of women's collective finds revealed through this myth. Their ideas were free from external influence. These were inherent qualities like virtues, because they're shaped by the group. A woman resigns herself to the fate, despite her own wisdom and truth. It can be cognized as a revolt against the social system. The myth justifies Hinduism as the way of life since time immemorial.

Notes

1. Kannur and Kasargod districts and parts of Kozhikode and Wayanad districts.
2. Theyyam performing castes of North Kerala.
3. Mazharul Islam, 1985 p. 385 *Folklore The Pulse of the People.*
4. Levi Straus 1978 p.19, 32. *Myth and Meaning.*
5. Indra Deva.1989. *Folk Culture and Peasant Society in India.*
6. Pallath, J.J. 1995. *Theyyam- An Analytical study of the folk culture wisdom and Personality.*
7. Amos, Dan Ben.1982. *Folklore in Context Essays.*
8. Islam, Mazharul. 1985 . *Folklore The Pulse of the People.*
9. Sahu, Nandini.2012.*Folklore and the Alternative Modernities.*
10. Corrupted word of Makkam Bhaghavati, the goddess Makkam.
11. Kadangode Makkam' along with her kids.
12. A Nair family at Kunhimangalam in Kannur, Kerala.
13. A caste name with lower status than Nair in the Hindu caste hierarchy with a traditional occupation of oil production. In Kerala social hierarchy based on caste were followed; Nambuthiris, Kshatriyas, Vaishyas and Shudras.

References

Amos, Dan Ben, 1982. *Folklore in Context Essays.* New Delhi: South Asian Publishers.

Bhatacharya, N.N.1977. *The Indian Mother Goddess.*New Delhi: Manohar Books.

Deva, Indra, 1989. *Folk Culture and Peasant Society in India.* Jaipur: Rawat Publications.

Frazer, James, 1976.*Golden Bough.* London: Mc Millan

Islam, Mazharul, 1985. *Folklore The Pulse of the People.* New Delhi: Concept Publishing Company.

Levi strauss, Claude, 1978. *Myth and Meaning.* London: Routledge & Kegan Paul.

Pallath, J.J. 1995.*Theyyam- An Analytical study of the folk culture wisdom and Personality.* New Delhi: Indian Social Institute.

Radcliffe Brown, A.R. 1952. *Structure and Function in Primitive Society.* London: Rotledge and Kegan Paul.

Sahu, Nandini, 2012. *Folklore and the Alternative Modernities.* New Delhi: Authors Press.

Sreedhara Menon, A. 1979. *Social and Cultural History of india.* New Delhi: Sterling Publishers.

Vasanthakumari, P. *Folklorile sthreeswatwanirmithi. Payyanur: FFM publications.*

15

Intangible Cultural Heritage and Sustainable Economic Development: A Case Of Pot Makers of Kannur District, Kerala

— *Sini. M*

Intangible cultural heritages are part of the traditional knowledge system and are an important element of nation building. UNESCO convention has defined Intangible cultural heritage as living cultural traditions, including oral traditions, performing arts, social practices, rituals, festive events, knowledge and practices concerning nature and the universe, or the knowledge and skills to produce traditional crafts (www.unesco.org/new). Amarasiri (2012) has defined the traditions which include oral, performing arts, rituals, festivals, craftsmanship etc., as intangible cultural heritage. As per Archibald (2004), intangible cultural heritage attempts to study and preserve cultural heritage in straight connection with the people/community of its origin. In short, Intangible cultural heritages are part of our identity.

Most communities in rural India are resource based communities. Their habitats determine their socio-economic life to a great extent. However, capacity building and resource mobilisation are essential for sustaining their tradition and societal structures. Generally, traditional knowledge systems are closed to external influences. Very often it is seen that external innovations and technology transfers are often accepted by community for endogenous development. It revolves around the traditional knowledge systems of the society. Therefore, it is imperative to reinforce the traditional knowledge systems and sustain cultural heritage and traditional economic sectors, especially craft sector since it is an important element of nation building.

Traditionally, craft depended communities were a crucial part of the village economy and heritage. However, most rural communities, especially the former struggle for survival and sustenance. For the socio-economic uplift of such communities and sustenance of their cultural heritage, creative and productive undertakings are essential. Integration of new technological aspects in the traditional socio-economic fabric of such community and their embellishments in tune with the modern day local demands might perhaps be the only way for the sustenance of the cultural heritage of these communities. Gizaw (2003) has pointed out that blending of technologies is a methodology through which social science will facilitate craftsmen to realize their powers, talents and aspirations.

Craft is an important part of intangible cultural heritage and also part of traditional economic sector. This sector has a crucial role in maintaining the tradition of a region. This is a part of village economy and informal production system. These were transmitted generation after generation. However, the pottery tradition in Kerala is a dying tradition today and is faced with the challenges of survival. It is mainly because, in most of the villages and rural areas, the pot makers are not aware of the changes happening and the new innovations to be absorbed in their arena and as a result they are mostly kept away from development possibilities. According to

Kreps (cited in Hennessy, 2010) objects stand for significant traditions, ideas, customs, social relations, and it is the story they tell, the performance they are a part of, and relationships among people and between people and places that are more important than the objects themselves. This reflects the inherent value of an object or entity in identity creation. Bala (2012) has pointed out that the Indians are losing their oral history, traditions and ICH at a very fast rate. He also mentioned that globalisation and modernisation have affected oral history and ICH. In this context, it is very important to conserve the traditional knowledge bases.

The tradition of pot making is at vanishing stage. Its safeguarding and revitalisation is a matter of exigency. The pot makers are part of our national cultural entity. It is very essential to craft it as a living heritage. For this, and for the sustainable development of pot makers and their tradition, preservation of traditional knowledge is essential. So, it is imperative to safeguard the intangible heritage. According to the UNESCO convention, not all the intangible heritages find safeguarded but only the one, recognised by its community as theirs providing them with a sense of identity and continuity that ought to be safeguarded.

In Kerala, the traditional pot makers were known in different names in different districts. Kannur and Kozhikode districts name them as Anthur Nairs, Palakkad as Kumbaran and as Velan in Thiruvananthapuram district. Odan, Kulalan, Andra Nair, Mannu Nair, Velar etc., are the other names. Generally, the terms Kusavan and Kulalan are used by the villagers to denote the pot makers of Kerala. In Kannur district, the Anthur Nairs are mainly distributed in twenty nine different settlements. The largest number of the population is found in Kannapuram and Tali paramba settlements (Sini 2004:101).

It is seen that the majority of Anthur Nairs were still dependent upon their traditional technology for the production process and were unaware of the new innovative and are faced with the challenges of survival. Creating awareness among them to cash in on their traditional knowledge and skills for strengthening the production process and value addition of products through the application of aesthetic and technological avenues with a global- local approach is vital. Thus, in addition to employment generation among the pot makers, the value addition of their products might be bringing international markets for their products.

The main challenges faced by the pot makers (Anthur Nairs) are,

- Lack of quality raw materials
- Outdated production methods
- Lack of skill upgradation and capacity building
- Lack of value addition of products
- Lack of adequate market linkages

To generate an expedient environment for the sustenance of cultural heritage and endogenous development of the community these aspects need to be addressed seriously and make them aware of the value with their expertise and cultural heritage. Capacity building and value addition of products makes the society productive and also preserves the cultural tradition. The Craft Council (1995) points out that no Indian craft is purely ever decorative.

For the sustenance of the community and preservation of ICH, the following key actions are essential:

- Impart training and capacity building on upgraded technology and innovations.
- Make certain the sustainable livelihood system of the community through the integration of traditional and modern/innovative technology.

- Make certain the value addition of their products and design upgradation.
- Assistance from development initiatives and promotional activities.
- Establish adequate market linkages.
- Cooperation between communities and various organisations.

Further, the documentation of such undertakings and initiatives would bring collective dealings from the people and community towards preservation and understanding of cultural heritage and also development of the community concerned.

Conclusion

It is imperative to promote and safeguard this cultural heritage as an asset for development. For this, linkages between traditional and modern practices are essential.

In order to maintain and achieve sustained development of traditional economic sectors especially craft sector and to safeguard the cultural heritage, investment and support in this locale is very essential. To withstand the future situations and remain sustainable, consistency, proficiency and resource mobilisation are very important.

References

Amarasiri, G D (2012). Safeguarding Sri Lanka's Intangible Cultural Heritage, Retrived from http:// archives.daily news/ 2012/06/27/fea0.5asp.

Archibald, R. 2014. The New Town Square; Museums and communities in Transition, Walnut Creek: Altamira Press.

Bala, Shashi. 2012. Digital inventories on Cultural memories on ICH: Case study of Yadav community of Haryana, India. Retrieved from http://network.icom. Museum /fileadmin/ user-upload/conferencepapers/2012/bala.pdf.

Crafts Council. 1995. A Report. New Delhi.

Gizaw, Berhanu. 2003. Blending of Traditional and Modern Technologies Through Science. International Conference on African Development Archives. Paper 67

Hennessy, Kate. 2010. Intangible Cultural Heritage Research and Documentation. Simon Fraser University, SIAT. Retrieved from http://www.sac.or.th /databases/ ichlearning resources/ images/ich-research-anddocumentationp1-50.pdf

Sini M 2004. Wheel technology and Pottery making tradition in Kerala: A Case study. Man and Life, 30: (3&4): 101-106. www.unesco.org/new Retrived 18.11.2014.

16

Mudiyettu, Kerala Ritual Dance

— Dr. V. Jayarajan

Mudiyettu, is a ritual dance drama symbolizing the mythical annihilation of *Darika,*[1] a demon by goddess *Bhadrakali*[2]. As a temple performance, *Mudiyettu* is in vogue mainly in Ernakulam, Thrissur and Kottayam districts and rarely in other places like Alleppey, and Idukki districts of Kerala, a southwestern state of India. It is also performed elsewhere, as the performing art. Literally, *Mudiyettu* means the wearing the headgear, symbolizing the coronation of Goddess *Bhadrakali,* the ferocious mother goddess. The impersonator of *Kali* adorns the huge crown making the whole atmosphere awe-inspiring. Though, the *Mudiyettu* is being performed with different rituals, lots of theatrical elements were also seen in its performance. The *Mudiyettu* performs in the temple premises of Kerala, as the ritual in between November and May with dates being apportioned in advance.

The mythology behind

Dwapara Yuga[3] witnessed fierce war between *Devas*[4] and *Asusras*[5]. Almost all *Asuras* except the four namely *Danamathi, Darumathi Vanika* and *Vamsika* were eliminated in the battle. *Danamathi* and *Darumathi* underwent deep penance to propitiate Lord *Brahma*[6] for a boon to protect

Asuras. Pleased by the penance Lord *Brahma* gave them boons for begetting offspring. Accordingly, two sons were born. They were *Danavendran* for *Danamathi* and *Darikan* for *Darumathi.* Two kingdoms namely *Darikapuri* and *Kapuram* were entrusted. Gradually, the *Asura* mothers narrated to their sons about the story of *Asuras*' defeat at the hands of *Devas* . *Danavendran* and *Darikan* were peeved against *Devas* and undertook severe penance in shallo water underneath besides in the midst of fire, in anticipation of Lord Brahma's mercy. They even cut their limbs and offered into a consecrated fire. After realizing the devotion of *Danavendran* and *Darikan,* Lord *Brahma* appeared before them and sought their vow. They besought boons for empowerment to decimate *Devas* in the battle front. Lord *Brahma* vouched them with anticipated boons. By the virtue of boons, when a drop of blood fell on earth, ten thousand *Maya Danavar* would sprout, with double strength of *Darikan.* They were each empowered of the might of sixteen thousand elephants. Another boon was that they were immune from any dare devil armed male during day or night. Lord Brahma gifted them with a war chariot. They were blessed with two *manthras*[7] namely *Viswapathi* and *Sahapathi* .

The duo became very powerful and arrogant. *Darikan* was on his misdeed even against Devas. He converted *Deva* women to *Asura* women. He dared Devas to fight against him. After realizing the boon of him not to be killed by male, *Devas* sent seven[8] powerful goddesses to fight against him. The blood spilled out of his body when used spears during their ambush. Eventually, thousands of *Darikas* were born. All the seven female deities were defeated in the battle. The victorious *Darika* went on harrassing the entire world and even the Gods. The sage *Narada*[9] was deputed to share the matter with Lord *Shiva.*[10] After hearing the misdeeds of *Darika,* Lord *Shiva* became infuriated and opened his fiery third eye. A huge and ferocious female deity *(Bhadrakali)* with sixteen hands emerged from his third eye. She was ordered to finish *Darika* . Sixteen weapons were apportioned to her.She was accompanied by *Bhutas*[11] and blood thirsty ghosts

When *Darika* saw *Bhadrakali* and her army ambushing towards him, he ignored them upon the boon of invincibility, but had forgotten that he could not be killed by women. A fierce battle ensued. The fight went on for a long time. *Bhadhrakali* was inflicted Smallpox during the course of the war. (The *Kali* performer's face has white pock marks as an indication of this cause) Finally, *Bhadrakali* eliminated him through chopping of his head. This is called *Darika Vadham*[12]. It is also considered as a victory of good over evil. A pictorial drawing of the Goddess *Bhadrakali* on the floor using color powder is also a part of the *Mudiyettu* ritual performance.

The Performance

The rituals pertaining to the *Mudiyettu* performance is complex in nature. Preparations such as certain vows are to be observed even days before. After the rituals in the shrines or temples *Kalamezhuthu*[13] starts either in the *mudippura*[14] or in the *pattupura.*[15] The goddess *Bhadrakali* finds being portrayed in two or three dimensional picture with severed head on one hand and different weapons on other hands. *Kurup*[16] or *Marar*[17] community draws the picture.

After finishing the drawing, *Kalam Pattu*[18] is performed. It is a narrative song related to the picture drawn on the floor. The percussion and wind instruments were the accompaniments of *kalam pattu.* It is believed that infuriated *Bhadrakali* was pacified after observing her portrait and hearing the song in adoration.

Mudiyettu, the ritual drama is apportioned into several scenes. It starts from *Kailasa,* the abode of Lord *Shiva* and from where the sage *Narada* meets Lord *Shiva*

and informs him about the misdeeds of duo - *Darika* and *Danavendra.*

Darika appears in the next scene. His arrogance and pride could be adjudged in the movements of the character. It is in the next scene namely Kali *Purappad*[19], Goddess *Kali,* the central character appears from the front of the temple. The impersonator adorning the crown is a sacred ritual in *Mudiyettu.* Jesters such as *Koyimpadanayar*[20] and *Kooli*[21] appear in the following scenes to bemuse the audience with jokes and comic actions.

The final battle between *Kali* and *Darika* follows. It is called *Koodiyattam.*[22] *Bhadrakali* uses sword, while *Darika* and *Danavendra* use dagger. In this fierce duel, *Asuras* were vanquished. They took refuge in the neither world - *Pathala*[23]. When she saw *Asuras,* running for life, *Kali*'s anger multiplied. *Koyimpadanayar* tries to cool her down by removing her headgear influencing her touch the ground with sword. When *Darika* and *Danavendra* came from the hide out, *Kali* behead them by chopping. She enters the arena with *Daraika* and *Danavendra*'s headgear symbolizing their death. The ritual continues even after slaying of *Darika- Danavendras.* Infants and children were picked by *Kali* from amidst spectators. They circumbulate the oil lamp placed in the front side. It is considered very auspicious and the children became immune from diseases.

Goddess *Kali* is being worshipped in almost all parts of Kerala state in different ways. In northern Kerala, it is in the form of *Theyyam,*[24] in the southern most districts, it is *kaliyoottu*[25], but it is *Padayani* elsewhere.[26] Local goddesses were being linked to *Bhadra Kali* cult. *Mudiyettu* is being performed in the villages to prevent the small pox as the epidemic is believed to be the wrath of Goddess *Kali.*

"*Mudiyettu* is considered to be a very powerful folk theatre of Kerala." folk theatre is the theatre which originated and evolved among, and has been transmitted through, the common people. Its relation with the common people is deep, and multilayered. It is a kind of entertainment but not the very entertainment. It carries the entire folk culture from within it with all its social and religious institutions.....sometimes, it takes the form of a ritual performed to propitiate divine forces for the welfare of the society and sometimes it is pure entertainment and simple" opines M.L Varadpande in the introduction of his book 'History of Indian Theatre'[27] The myth and style of performance, the involvement and active participation of the public demonstrate the continuity of the age old tradition and the transmission of moral values to future generations. *Mudiyettu* carries forward the tradition of *Bhadrakali* worship, as it is being believed to be the triumph of good over evil.

An ICH element

Mudiyettu is a performance with lots of rituals, music, dance and drama. It is a complex cultural expression with knowledge, belief, art, morals, and custom. Its close connection to fertility cult is obvious as the performance takes place after the harvest. Offering paddy seeds to mother goddess is a custom followed by the villagers dancing around the temple. Bringing the Goddess ceremoniously from the paddy fields to the temple is also conducted as a part of the *Mudiyettu* festival. Moreover, *Mudiyettu* is considered as a thanks giving ceremony for begetting bountiful crops. Arena is decorated with agricultural produce. Paddy and rice are being considered to be the main ingredient s for performance. Almost all old shrines situated either in the paddy fields or near to it. Another interesting feature is that all the *Mudiyettu* performing temples lie on the banks of three major rivers of Kerala. They are *Chalakkudy, Periyar* and *Moovattupuzha.* There were around hundred shrines or temples in Kerala, which host the performance, once a year.

Mudiyettu is performed by very few families and groups of Kerala. There were mainly two communities behind the performance - *Marar* and - *Kurup*. Now, there are about ten groups[28] performing *Mudiyettu*. They are-

1. Varanattu Mudiyettu Sanagam, Koratty, Thrissur
2. Varanattu SankaranarayanaKuruppu Mudiyettu Kalakendram, Koratty, Thrissur.
3. Varanattu SankaraKuruppu Mudiyetty sangam, Koratty, Thrissur.
4. Shree Shankarankutty Smaraka Mudiyettu sangam, Keezhillam, Perumbavoor.
5. Shree Pazhoor Damodaramarar Smaraka Gurukulam, Mudiyettu Sangam, Moovattu puzha.
6. Shree Punayakkal Kunhan Marar Mudiyettu Kalakendram, Tirumarayoor, Eranakulam
7. Shree Badra samajam Mudiyettu sangam, Udayamperoor, Eranakulam
8. Shree Rudra Mudiyettu Sangam Mudiyettu sangam, Kuttumanoor, Puthankurisu, Eranakulam
9. Mudiyettu Sangam, Maradi
10. Mudiyettu Sangam, Kunnaykkal, Valakam

The above performing groups belong to Eranakulam and Thrissur districts. Out of the above ten groups, the descendants of three traditional performing families dominate in the performance. They pass the tradition from one generation to another on regular basis in temples as they hold traditional right over such performance [patented one]. They are –

1. Pazhoor Damodar Marar Smaraka Gurukulam, Eranakulam
2. Shankaran Kutty Marar Smaraka Gurukulam, Keezhillam and
3. Varanattu family Mudiyettu Sangam (Now they split into two more groups)

As Mr Keezhillam Unnikrishnan[29], aged 43 points out, he started performing this art form right from his childhood. He claims him to be the fourth generation artist Unnikrishnan learnt *Mudiyettu* from his father, Shankaran kutty Marar, who was considered as one among the great *Mudiyettu* artistes of Kerala. Unnikrishnan had several occasions to accompany his father in the entourage for performance. He started performing on the stage, when he was barely ten year old. At the age of 25, he performed the prestigious role of Kali. He has completed around 1,000 *Kali* characters on different stages.

Mudiyettu underlines the Indian traditional theatrical concept. It had had three elements such as dance, song and rhythm involved. It is called *Touratrikam* [30]in Indian theatrical concept. The *kalamezhuthu* (drawing of goddess *Kali*'s figure) represents three aesthetic elements they are *Chitravadivu*[31], *shilapavadivu*[32] and *Bhoota vadivu*[33].

Conclusion

Mudiyettu was inscribed in the Representative List of Intangible Cultural Heritage of Humanity by UNESCO [after thoroughly scrutinizing the merits] - 2010 as per the decision of 5.COM 6.17.After the inscription in the representative list of ICH of humanity, *Mudiyettu* became more popular amongst the national and international audience. Moreover, the inscription could raise awareness about the significance of Intangible Cultural Heritage by offering an example of social harmony among different castes and communities;

Apex bodies of Cultural Department such as *Sangeet Natak Akademy* and *Indira Gandhi National Centre for the Arts* have hosted the performances. The artistes, especially the youngsters were inspired by the UNESCO Declaration bringing more youngsters into *Mudiyettu* performance. Invitations for performance have come even from abroad. One such performance was held at Korean National

University of Arts, Seoul on October 9th and 20th, 2015. *A Mudiyettu* team was led by Keezhillam Unnikrishnan at Seoul. It was followed by the workshop cum demonstration. Dr. V. Jayarajan, chairman, Folkland.

Reference

1. Achutha Menon, Chelanattu, Keralathile Kali Seva (Mal) Madras University, Madras 1943.
2. Chandra Hasan K.A, Padayani, Mudiyettu, Theeyattu (Mal) Impact, Tripunithura 1989.
3. Chummar Choondal, Mudiyettu, (Mal) Kerala Folklore Academy, Thrissur 1981.
4. Chummar Choondal - Studies in folklore of Kerala, college Book house Trivandrum 1978.
5. Dr. C.R. Rajagopalan, Mudiyettu, Nadodi Nerarangu, Ascend Publications, Kottayam 2015 Gundert Nighandu. DC Books - Kottayam 1995.
6. Keezhillam Unnikrishnan, Namavaseshmakunna Nadan kalakal (Mal) Ernakulam 2010.
7. Raghavan Pillai K (Ed) Kalee Natakam(Mal) Kerala University, Trivandrum 1960.
9. Thirumulpad.P.K -Mudiyettu enna Anushtana Natakam, (Mal) Kothamangalm 1993.
10. K.N Panikker, Folklore of Keral NBT, New Delhi 1991.
11. Venu.G. Puppetry and Lesser known Dance traditions of Kerala Natanakairali, Irinjalakuda 1990.
12. V. Jayarajan, Teyyam, A divine Dance tradition of Kerala, IGRMS, Bhopal 2008 and internet sources.

Notes

01. An Asura, who got an immunity by Lord Brahma from being killed by men and weapons.
02. A Hindu goddess associated with empowerment.
03. Yuga is an epoch or era in Hindu mythology. Among the four Yugas Dwapara Yuga is the third one. Others are Satya Yuga, Treta Yuga and Kali Yuga.
04. Heavenly, divine, terrestrial things of high excellence, exalted, shining ones. The concept also used to refer to deities.Devas represent the good.
05. Supernatural beings. Asuras represent the evilness.

06. God of creation in Hinduism
07. A hymn with magic powers.
08. Bhramani, Vaishnavi, Maheswari, Kaumari, Indrani, Varahi, and Chamundi were the seven goddesses.
09. Narada is a Vedic sage, who played the role as messenger and mediator in Hindu mythology.
10. One among the three main deities of Hinduism. It is also known as the God of destroyer.
11. Celestial attendants.
12. Killing of Darika.
13. The drawing of Goddess Kali using indigenous color powder on the floor.
14. The sacred place where Goddess Kali's Crown is kept.
15. The place from where deities are invoked by singing songs.
16. A temple servant community whose main occupation is drawing the picture of Gods and Goddesses in temples.
17. The temple musician community.
18. Singing mythical songs to invoke the deity.
19. Tjhe entry of Kali.
20. A clown character.
21. A Mischievous spirit.
22. The dancing together.
23. Hades.
24. A Vibrant ritual dance.
25. A temple performance depicting the fight between Kali and Darika.
26. A ritual performance vogue in Quilon, Pathanamthitta, Allepey and Kottyam districts of Kerala.
27. The History of Indian theatre- 1996, New Delhi.
28. Dr. C.R. Rajagopalan, Mudiyettu- Nadodi nattarangu, pp. 135, Kottayam 2015.
29. A leading performer and leader of Shankaran Kutty marar Smarka Keezhillam
30. It contains three elements.
31. The pictorial perfection
32. The sculptural perfection
33. The spiritual perfection

17

Arundhathiyars of Puducherry

— *Dr. V. Pragati*

The anthropologists study religion in different perspective and it is entirely different. They focus only upon its social perspective and cultural setting. The religion is a part and parcel of culture. They give importance to its congregational, the functional and the societal aspect of religion. The religion, in short, is some belief in supernatural or spiritual beings, as it consists of beliefs and rites. It is the human response, expression and relation to the uncompromising, uncontrollable phenomena and forces of nature. The scholarly studies on religion paved way to any Indian and European anthropologists to do research on various aspects of religious and belief practices of rural and tribal people. Scholars like Srinivas, (1965), Hassan(1967), Jacob-Pandian, (1975), Babb (1975), Wadley (1975), Thurston (1975), Appadurai and Breckenridge (1976), Moffat, Michael (196I), Inden (1976), Clothey (1978),Ostor (1980), Fuller (1982), (1992), Kjaerholm (1984), (1992), Dumont (1986), (1909), Nishimura, Yuko (1987),Whitehead (1988), (1921); Raheja (1988), Rao, (1991), Ayyer(1992), Nobokov (1995), Petitet, and Pragathi, (2007), and have demonstrated such fusions were accomplished by reciprocal relations. This paper presents on the socio-religious aspect of Puducherry

Arundhathiyar in the village settings. In Puducherry, now the Union Territory, there were about fifteen types of Scheduled Caste. *Arundhathiyar* belong to Scheduled Caste community and they got migrated to Southern part of Tamil Nadu and Puducherry long way back some centuries ago. *Arundhathiyar* of Tamil Nadu and Puducherry were migrants from Andhra Pradesh. They migrated to Puducherry from neighbouring states in the 17th century. The *Arundhathiyars* were identified by the names of *Madiga* and *Chakkiliyan* in the Census 2011. Their mother tongue was Telugu, but now bilinguals, as they were good in communicating through Telugu and Tamil languages. They could speak their mother tongue with kids, family members and relatives, despite settling selves in Tamil Nadu. The *Chakkiliyan* believe that they have descended from *Arundhathi* star, the star, who was the consort of sage *Vasishta.* And so, they like to be called as *Arundhathiyar,* and it gives them prestigious status. The *Chakkiliyan* of Puducherry Union Territory has changed their name as *Arundhathiyar,* as this name is being considered more respectable than the original names. It endorses them a relatively better status among other Scheduled Castes/ other communities.

The *Arundhathiyar* claims them being spatially the most widespread Scheduled Caste groups in India. They have distributed across the state of erstwhile Andhra Pradesh, Tamil Nadu, Karnataka, Kerala, Maharashtra and Orissa. They were known as *Madiga* in Andhra Pradesh, and *Chakkiliyan* in Tamil Nadu and Kerala. They were known by other names, such as *Matangulu, Kattimadiga, Madiga, Pedda Madiga, Edagaiyavaru, Jambuvalu, Manjigoolu* and *Chakkiliyar,* in Andhra Pradesh, Tamil Nadu and Puducherry and they belong to left hand caste group. Their staple foods are rice and ragi. They eat all types of non-vegetarian food. They eat fowls, pork, beef, and varieties of fish. Most of the men drink country liquor and toddy, but bottled liquor, very rarely. Their consumption of milk and its products is very low. They are leather workers, carcass removers, tanners, footwear maker, drum beaters and were agricultural labourers. . They usually erect huts either in the government land or in the outskirts of the village. However, some of them got houses constructed by the government.

In a particular area, a group of families were assigned where in they play some key role on certain occasions like village festivals, death ceremonies social and religious functions. The *Arundhathiyar* men beat drums and play flute during death and other socio-religious functions. They messenger in advance about the dates of festivals, village functions etc. They rear pigs and sell its meat (pork) in villages, as well as in weekly markets. Domestic animals such as country pigs, hens and dogs were also reared. All their sons share the property equally after their father. The *Arundhathiyars* family reveals that as any were else, joint family system finds extinct. Traditional joint families were not as large as in the mainstream of Indian society. Nearly two-thirds of the sample respondent's live in nuclear families leaving about a third in joint families.

Arundhathiyars were endogamous and clear exogamous lineage groups were being identified. Uncle-niece marriages, cross-cousin marriages (in the form of a man marrying his father's sister's daughter and mother's brother's daughter) were highly preferred. Monogamy is common, but polygyny is being permitted, in case, the first wife is sterile or suffers from chronic illness. Though marriages are fixed through negotiation and mutual consent, other marriages, such as elopement and love were common. Toe rings and *bottu tali*, on a turmeric stained string, were the marriage symbols for any woman. It is a patriarchal society and patrilocal residence is the norm. After marriage, the couples live with boy's parents for some time, and some live separately, at later stage. However, the majority were being joint families. The kinship is descriptive and they use specific terms to refer to their members. The *Arundhathiyars* observe pre-delivery rituals for pregnant women. Her parents give her *arachoru* in the fifth month of pregnancy. In the seventh or ninth month, a ceremony called *valaikaappu*[1] (pregnancy) ceremony is being performed; wherein the elderly women adorn the hands of the pregnant woman with glass bangles. They observe birth pollution for nine days. On ninth day, the mother and infant were given purification bath. This is known as *tiTTu kalikaradhu*[2]. The child is then placed in the cradle and naming ceremony takes place on the same day. The ear–boring and tonsuring ceremonies are performed in the family deity (*kulatyvam*) temples; when the child will be three or five years of age. When a girl attains puberty, she is secluded and made seated in a corner of the house on a mat. Her pollution period lasts for seven days. On the seventh day, she is given ritually purification bath and a small ritual is performed within the family members. Some families give a banquet on the occasion. The *Arundhathiyar* bury the dead. The eldest son conducts the funeral rites for father and the 3 youngest for mother. The death entails pollution for 11 days and *karumaati*[3] is performed on the last day. A small non-vegetarian feast is served. Some families remember the departed souls and offer new clothes for the departed, in a symbolic fashion on important festival days.

Religion among *Arundhathiyar* plays an important role. It unites them in their individual capacity on one belief and rituals. *Arundhathiyars* believe family gods and goddesses. They are highly religious, and very much afraid of supernatural powers. *Arundhathiyar* believe that their community be obliged to Lord *Siva* and Lord *Vishnu*. These have been the faces of metaphysical arguments, as the two main streams of Hindu religion i.e., *Siva*, the school of *Saivism* and *Vaishnava*, the school of *Vaishnavism* found among *Arundhathiyar*. The entire *jati* of Puducherry *Arundhathiyars* finds apportioned into *vamsams* namely *bujakoolu* and *naamakoolu*. These divisions were based on the *Saivite* (*bujakoolu*) and *Vaishnaivite* (*naamakoolu*) divisions. They follow different customs, while performing the rites and rituals. The *vamsams* i.e., *bujakoolu* and *naamakoolu* are being further sub-divided into five *gotrams*, again being classified into several *kulams*.

The Worship of Gods

Let us begin with God worship. The *Arundhathiyars* were strong believers in simple devotion of gods and goddesses. Their devotion is expressed in worshipping different gods. Their main figures were found to have inspired and animated their souls through the ages, and still inspiring are Lord *Siva* and *Vishnu*. They value Lord *Siva* and *Vishnu* equally a capable of giving supernatural rewards. The three-fold marks, as stated early, visible on the forehead of *Arundhathiyars* are the symbols of the popular gods. The horizontal lines marked with ashes represent their devotion of Lord *Siva* and are known as *bujakoolu*. The *bujakoolu vamsam* is divided into three *gotrams*, namely, *bujakoolu*, *pandibujakoolu*, and *lingabujakoolu*. The vertical sandal paste in white signifies their faith in Lord *Vishnu* and is known as *naamakoolu*. The *naamakool vamsam*, is divided into two *gotrams* namely *padamleni naamakoolu* and *padam petina naamakoolu*. *Padamleni naamakoolu* put single vertical line with chalk on their forehead and *padam petina naamakoolu* put with chalk single vertical line and in the end horizontal line. In any social and religious rituals, the first and foremost God worshipped is Lord *Pullari*[4] (Lord *Vighnesvara*). They begin the ritual by offering prayers to Lord *Pullari*. They light incense sticks and camphor and then break open a coconut. Generally, whether in the performance of religious acts, or life-cycle ceremonies, or the building of houses and the like, initial prayers were offered to Lord *Pullari*, to overcome obstacles and remove arising difficulties.

The Worship of Goddess

The Goddess has great importance in the religious life of *Arundhathiyars*. They are being worshipped occasionally, on ear-boring, tonsuring, marriage and other religious occasions. *Arundhathiyars* worship the following Goddesses (*devataikal*) in order to achieve their different ends in life. Lord *Brahma's* wife *Saraswati* is the Goddess of learning and Lord *Vishnu's* wife Lakshmi is the Goddess of wealth and prosperity. Along with these Goddesses of great tradition, they also worship *Mariyamman, Ankalamman, Paaliriciyamman* and *Kannimar*. Their belief in the Goddesses is very strong. The community members worship them, as this act protects the village from sickness, epidemics and evil spirits. *Mariyamman, Ankalamman,* and *Paaliriciyamman* were represented by a black-stone; and an iron rod spear finds placed next to the idol. Nearby the *Arundhathiyar* village, there is a *Chakkili mariatta* temple. In South Indian temples, snake hoods were underneath the margoosa tree, *azadirachta indica* (*veepamaram*[5]) and banyan tree, *ficusbengalensis* (*alamaram*).

The village Gods *Aiyanaar:*

This god is regarded to be the son of the *Siva* and *Vishnu.* Actually, he is an old Dravidian divinity. *Aiyanaar* temple is in the outskirts of the village. He is guardian of the fields and the armed protector of the village's territory.

Madurai-viiran:

The secondary divinity, fearsome a carnivorous, alcohol-drinking god. They usually offer a pig. They say that *madurai viiran* is our god.

The Kulatyvam (Family deity)

Among *Arundhathiyars,* there were deities (inherited) which were referred to as family deity, (*kulatyvam*) and were enshrined in a corner of the house. Worshiping of family deities is compulsory during life-cycle ceremonies and religious occasions. The family deity (*kulatyvam*) a highly traditional form of worship, closely linked to the lineage and guarded possession. The entire lineage members were involved during such worship. Any failure will harm the members of the family. Vows (*prarttanai*) were made to redress the grievances. If the vows were unfulfilled, the family deities were supposed to harm them make them to suffer with serious health issues or cause to death.

Ancestral Spirits

At the family level, every *Arundhathiyar* worships his own ancestors, enshrined in the middle house (*nattuviittu*) and usually located near the cooking hearth in the north eastern corner of the house. In the middle house (*nattuviittu*), underneath the deities' photos, a circle is drawn with turmeric paste on the wall and three horizontal lines were put with vermilion interspersed by dots. While offering prayers (*puccai*) to the deities either at home or at the shrine, the ancestors were also worshipped. The family gather for the occasion usually including those who ever lived with deceased–parents, siblings, children, and in-laws. Around mid-morning, they gather near the ritual centre of the household, and perform special ritual to the ancestors. During life-cycle rituals like childbirth and marriage, ancestors worship is purely obligatory. Any negligence in offerings and sacrifices or any polluted person entering *nattuviittu*, the ancestral spirits assault family members. Usually, they protect and guard the family from unforeseen situations in their bid to facilitate their future generations. They were therefore, venerated and propitiated by the family. Therefore, it is the duty of the head of the family to keep the ancestors pleased and be favourable by worshipping them on several occasions during the year, viz., *diiwali, nattu-karitikai, mattu-ponkal,* childbirth and marriage. In other words, when they observe any festivities and happy occasions, they worship the ancestors by suitable offerings and sacrifices.

Malevolent Spirits

The malevolent spirits, which are evil in character and do harm to human beings on malicious whims were termed as the evil–spirits (*peey-picacu*), and wind-spirits (*kattu-karuppu*) are so powerful that they might kill human beings. The latter were supported to dwell in the graveyard or in the old temples. Persons, who die unnatural death, or by accidents, death by hanging, falling from a tree, suicide or murder, were believed to become the malevolent spirits, these spirits were supposed to be invisible and cause diseases or death, if anyone unknowingly passes by such tree alone. These deaths were viewed as contaminated and looked with fear and awe, and therefore lengthy and complicated purification rites are being prescribed for such unnatural deaths. In almost all parts of mountains and forests, some kind of malefic spirits were believed to exist. Therefore, they were propitiated at the time of worship of trees and plants. The giant trees, like palm tree, *arecaceae* (*panamaram*) or margoosa tree, *azadirachtaindica* (*veepamaram*), are the habitat of spirits known by the term *muni or muniiswaran*[6] and *katteeri*[7].

Sun and Moon Worship

The worship of sun and moon is also popular among the *Arundhathiyars,* generally Tuesdays and Fridays, especially on lunar junctures of new moon (*amavacai*) and full moon (*paurrnami*) light. New moon (*amavacai*) day is celebrated in the honour of ancestors particularly, the day of new moon is celebrated in the months *of Adi, Purattaci* and *Tai* in honour of ancestors is most importantly celebrated by all the families. *Paurrnami* (full moon) ceremonies are also connected with rebirth, especially a new life, while those of the new moon are associated with death and funeral aspects (Bhattacharyya, 1977: 288).

Hence, life–cycle ceremonies were performed during full moon (*paurrnami*) time. The popular belief that this ceremony is to be performed during a bright night is thus widespread among women in Tamil Nadu.

Temple Worship

Besides, these informal worships, they offer *puccai* to different deities, installed them in a temple. Temples of Lord *Vishnu* are spread in the area. Almost all the villages have Lord *Sivan* temple, where *puccai* is offered every day. They also go to distant temples situated 10 or 20 Kms away from the village, across the Puducherry region.

Pilgrimage

Most often they go to pilgrimage centres in southern and northern parts of Tamil Nadu. They undertake special vows for certain things and go for pilgrimage to Lord *Venkateswara* temple, Tirupathi temple in Andhra Pradesh, Meel Malaiyanuur temple, *Ankaalaparameecuvari temple* and Lord *Murgan* temple at Palani hills in Tamil Nadu, and Lord *Ayyappa*, Sabiramala temple in Kerala, to fulfil their vows. For both *drishti*[8] and *dosham*[9], they take infants to Muslim mosque. The *Bhai* is a Muslim priest in the *Dargaah/Masudhi* (*Mosque*) and he acts as a healer. He recites mantras (*mantiram*) by waving with peacock feathers over the face of the baby and ties a red knotted string or talisman (*sevappu mantriicha kairu*[10]/ *mudi kairu*) to the baby's hand. They also bring enchanted water (*mantriicha thanni*) from the *Dargaah / Masudhi* (*Mosque*). This charged water is used to wash the face and is given the baby to drink. They take the sick child to the Hindu Gods/Goddesses temples, worship and do special *puccai* in its name.

Animal Worship

Cow and Cobra occupies an important place in *Arundhathiyar*. Cow is being worshipped in natural or normal death anniversaries. During *mattu ponkal* festival the cows were being decorated and worshipped. Cobra deity is better understood as responsible for human procreation as the god and goddess of fertility, that is, *Nagappa-Nagamma* or *Nagaathamman,* seen as the bestowal of fertility. Infertile *Arundhathiyar* women pray to the idols of *Nagappa-Nagamma* depicted in sexual embrace, hoping to conceive.

Trees Worship

The trees and plants like margoosa tree, *azadirachta indica* (*veeppamaram*), pipal tree, *ficus religiosa* (*aracamaram*), banyan tree, *ficus bengalensis* (*alamaram*) and holi basil, *ocymum sanctum* (*tulasi*) is commonly considered sacred and worshipped among the *Arundhathiyars.* These trees and plants were planted in the backyard/courtyard of *Arundhathiyars* households. The margoosa tree, *azadirachta indica* (*veepamaram*) is associated with the virgin goddess *Mariyamman* and is believed to ward off evil effects and purify the atmosphere (Nishimura, 1987). These trees and plants occupy an important place in magic and medicine, which they believe and apply accordingly. The *Arundhathiyar* women worship the margoosa tree, *azadirachta indica* (*veepamaram*) on Tuesdays and Fridays by smearing it with turmeric, *curcuma longa* (*manjal*) and vermillion (*kunkumam*). A string of mango tree, *mangifera indica* (*maamaram*) and margoosa tree, *azadirachta indica* (*veepamaram*) leaves are pinned as *thoranam* across the lintel of the threshold, during any social and religious ritual. Mango tree, *mangifera indica* (*maamaram*), like the whole tree itself, is very potent 'multifocal' or 'multivalent' (Turner, 1967) symbolic import in the religious system of the Tamil and other Southern India. It symbolizes with fertility, fruitfulness and coolness. These are being the strong values antipathetic to the polluting, deathly forces which pervade uncivilised areas.

Nagappa-Nagamma is seen as bestowals of fertility, *Arundhathiyar* women, who believe selves to be infertile, pray to them in their sexual embrace, hoping to conceive. Small shrine to this composite Cobra deity stands under a scared pipal tree, *ficus religiosa* (*arasamaram*) in every village. Most Snake god images are being installed under sacred trees (especially margoosa tree, *azadirachta indica* (*veepamaram*), pipal tree, *ficus religiosa* (*arasamaram*), and banyan tree, *ficus bengalensis* (*alamaram*) in the open–air courtyard of temples. They will receive their worship in this leafy environment, although snake stones are located at the side of roads, near anthills. There is always a small shrine to *Pillaiyar* (G*anesa/ Vinayak*) aside, as the divine Remover of Obstacles. Barren Women (*malati*) circle the sacred tree with sacred images and pray before them, especially to that of the Cobra deity. The idols were smeared with, sandal paste *santalum album* (*cantanam*), turmeric powder, *curcuma longa* (*manjal*) and vermilion (*kunkumam*) and then they go around the trees 108 times.

Gods and Diseases

The *Arundhathiyars* believe that for maintaining general health and well being, the goodwill of gods and goddesses is quite essential. So they propitiate them and also make periodical offerings to maintain their pleasure. Gods' are generally benevolent in nature, but turn malevolent when people provoke them through evil deeds. The angry gods will send diseases and other calamities to people to punish them. *Mariyamman* is one of the chief goddesses who get angry easily. She will cause skin diseases, fever and belly pain, besides small pox, chicken pox and measles. The pox diseases such as smallpox (*periya ammai*), chickenpox (*chinaammai*), measles (*thata ammai*), corriander pox (*kothamali ammai*) and mums (*thondai ammai*) are attributed to *Mariyamman* (mother goddess). This epidemic constitute a special category, as all of them are supposed to because by the wrath of goddess

Mariyamman. Her common name in Tamil Nadu is *Mariyamman*. A majority of the prefixes to the names just catalogued have to do with small pox. So the identity of the deity appears by that to be fixed. The *Muniiswaran* can attack a person of any age and sex. Then the *mantravaati* can rescue such person from his attack. He will invoke some benevolent deities toward the *Muniiswaran* off. The patient will be cured of the illness following the expulsion of *Muniiswaran* from body sheath. Some of the evil-spirits (*peey-picacu*) and wind-spirits (*kattu-karuppu*) can cause accidents to people, while they roam in the wild forests. These two malevolent spirits *Muniiswaran* and *Katteeri*, particularly harm the pregnant and newly delivered woman; hence *puccai* is performed on the behalf of them. They do a small *puccai* to appease those spirits. After offering prayers to concerned spirits the sanctified food (*prasadam*) is given to the pregnant woman, newly delivered woman, and to the rest of the family members. The *puccai* is performed to them in order to protect the pregnancy of woman and to have safe delivery.

Religious Beliefs for Wellbeing

In *Arundhathiyars* life, religion plays an important role in all spheres of their life. Even in health care religious beliefs and practice have their own specific influence?. They derive the cause of many of supernatural forces, that they play direct role in the causation and cure of many of such diseases. They believe some cordial relation with the deities and ancestral spirits could ensure good health for the members of the community. So, they perform ceremonies every year during annual festivals, to renew their relation with supernatural entity for the protection of the hamlet. To fulfil the wishes, they take different vows such as, *kaavadi* bearing. The word itself appears to be the combination of two words *kaavu* and *adi* intended to mean the vow made to walk the distance to the place of pilgrimage on foot. There are different kinds of this *kaavadi* and of which, three were worth mentioning. There is one going by the name of *anna kaavadi.* The devotees go to the house to house "house begging" for cooked rice not with the idea of satisfying his/her own hunger, but to offer the gathering to God. An offering to God generally means an offering to humanity. Hence, the vow of taking *anna kaavadi* is really a vow to beg food from others, door-to-door and place-to place, to offer the same to the hungry and needy in God's name. The second kind of *kaavadi* is called the *paal kaavadi,* the vow of begging milk from house-to-house to be utilised in the service of God. Usually, the milk so collected is poured upon the image of the deity, collected again in a vessel and disposed of either by distributing among the children, or by utilizing the same for satisfying personal hunger and demand. The third kind of *kaavadi* is perhaps the one observed by people without the possibility of its degenerating into selfish use. It consists in making a vow that is he/she would undertake pilgrimage to the one or the other of the temples, to worship the deity. It is nothing but the offering of devotee's energy to the deity, by means of walking to the temple. They carry an object called *kaavadi* in the form of a segment of a circle made, decorated and carried with great veneration to install in the mind of the observer, as the needed right spirit. People used to make such vows. Certain offering shall be made to particular god for getting a favour in return. Any failure on his/her part to avow against received favour, the infuriated will curse to suffer from incurable diseases as the mode of punishment.

The Sacred Specialists

The ritual functionaries, who do sacred performances, are known as "sacred specialists". Among the *Arundhathiyars*, the latter were found at two levels, one at the family level and other at the village level. The head of the family acts as the sacred specialist to perform family level religious functions. There were certain taboos, such as observance of strict fast on the day of worship, and asceticism for a week. The chieftain of the family cannot act as sacred specialist and perform the rites during ritual functions, if his wife is under periods, and also, any accrual of ritual impurity from the inevitable death or birth. The sacred specialist decides the dates of sacred performances only after considering those factors, subject to the convenience of every member of his lineage, which were the co-shares of such worship. The other important sacred specialist is the village temple priest. Usually, each settlement of the *Arundhathiyar* will have one or two shrines of Gods with worshipping priests. The latter does the sacred performances in the shrine, he functions also as a man prophesying about the future, curing diseases and warding spirits off that possess the individuals and some priests, were also diviners. The sacred specialist at the village level is bound to fallow same inhibitions, as the family level sacred specialist follow during religious functions.

Sacred Performances

The sacred performances can be similarly categorised into those at the family level, village level, and festivals and magical performances. They are being invoked and propitiated by performing several rituals like worship, prayer, making vows, offering vegetarian and non-vegetarian food etc. Such offerings and sacrifices were being made ensuring health, happiness, prosperity and plenty of food supply to the people in return. The rituals can be considered as sacred performances. The objectives of which were clear. The Gods and Goddesses bless without any volition, unless elaborate rituals appease them. Even spirits ought to be satisfied and any failure could invite harmful consequences. The benevolent spirits may not harm much for the subject unable to perform any particular ritual, but the displeased evil spirits shower disease or death for the defaulters.

Offerings made to the Deities

The material requirements in various rites and rituals are being standardized. The *puccai* performing place is sanctified and smeared with cowdung and finds later decorated with banana leaves, mango twigs and flowers. The worshipping, propitiation and celebration of deities consists of two types of offerings, such as animal flesh foods and articles such as cooked rice, coconuts, bananas, camphor, incense sticks, flowers, earthen lamps, winnowing basket, husked rice, liquor, vermilion and turmeric, *curcuma longa* (*manjal*) powder. The animals sacrificed to the deities were the he goats, he-pigs and cocks. The kinds of offerings made to the deities depend upon the occasion, the ritual and the food habits of the deity receiving those offerings. The animal offerings were made by the individual families and also collectively by the entire community.

Conclusion

The beliefs and practices of the *Arundhathiyar* regarding supernatural beings show the devotion and anxiety of such brethren at the level of socio-cultural integration. The religious life of *Arundhathiyars* analysed with the help of three methodological terms, viz., sacred centres, sacred specialists and sacred performances, if conceived together may be termed as "the sacred-complex". The sacred centres of the *Arundhathiyars* were located at a number of places, viz., in the house, courtyard, cattle shed within settlement, or outskirts of the village, and in the neighbouring places. The deities enshrined were represented by stones or rocks of different colours, trees, spears, iron rods and trident. Practically no significant change is perceptible in the religious and ritualistic behaviour of the *Arundhathiyars*. The impact of technological and modern materialistic culture has not been as powerful, as that of religious culture on the *Arundhathiyars*. Worships and other religious acts are part and parcel of their daily life. However, the so-called modern and sophisticated youngsters seldom conform to such ideals, though the old and the aged hang on to them. Lastly, it is concluded that the *Arundhathiyars*, like most other castes of Puducherry attach prime importance to religious practices in every lifestyle. Human life as perceived by them is full of hazards; they should seek the help of supernatural beings. *Arundthathiyar* of Puducherry presents a colourful panorama of religious faiths and practices, which is the manifestation of adjustments with cultural-ecological conditions. It conceives man as passing through a life surrounded by the evil-spirits (*peey-picacu*) and wind-spirits (*kaatu-karupu*) company of powers and elements, mostly impersonal in their character. Some of these were regarded as presiding forces' over various departments of life, each force having the sphere of influence. These were diligently propitiated to ward–off inevitable dangers associated with influence.

Notes

1. *Valaikaappu*: They take a special note of a Woman's first pregnancy: *valaikaappu* or *cul kaappu* (talismanic bangle ceremony) is performed by all irrespective of any economic status, to ensure that the woman will give birth in the happy mood of the *valaikaappu* celebration. Hence, this ceremony is being celebrated in the seventh or ninth month of the pregnancy (Petitet and Pragathi, 2007). In *valaikaappu* the *valayal* is a noun from the verb *valai,* which means to surround; hence, *valayal* may be taken to mean an ornament to surround the wrist and *kaappu* means an amulet.
2. *tiTTu kalikaradhu.*: Purification ceremony is known as *tiTTu kalikaradhu.* It marks the end of the period of potential pollution and is the final cleansing act before the re-integration into the society.
3. *Karumaati:* After funeral the concluding death ceremony takes place on thirteenth or sixteenth day. In Tamil language it is known as *karumaati.*
4. *Pullari* or *Pillari:* It is the colloquial name of Lord *Vighnesvara,* also called *Pilliyaar, Ganesh* and *Vinaayakar.* In Tamil country,

pillai means "child" and *pillaiyaar* "noble child"; it probably originally meant "the young one of an elephant" (Bagchi, 1998).We encountered the term *Pullari* rather than *Pillari* in our fieldwork.

5. *Veepa eelai* (margoosa leaves, *azadirachta indica*): *veepa eelai* (margoosa leaves, *azadirachta indica*), are believed to be auspicious and are used for medical purposes. Margoosa is also associated with the virgin goddess *Mariyamman,* and is believed to ward off evil effects and purify the atmosphere.
6. *Muniiswaran*: *Muniiswaran* is an important evil spirit causing a lot of hardship to the people.
7. *Katteeri: Katteeri* who was widely known to be the ghost of a woman who had died in the pregnancy (or childbirth) and now vented her frustration on women, snatching their unborn babies and small children (Caplan, 1987; Fuller, 1992).
8. *Drishti:* The evil-eye attack is locally by termed as *drishti.* It is the malignant power of the evil eye exercised by human beings.
9. *Dosham* (astrological danger): "Problems" in a horoscope are called "*dosham*". This multivalent word (meaning fault, flaw, danger, sin) is generally understood, in the Tamil astrological context, to connote dangers in a horoscope. These *dosham* abode is an inauspicious future.
10. *Mantricha kairu*: Muslim priest of *Mosque* do special prayers and enchants some *mantras,* finally gives red thread i.e., *mantricha kairu* and ties it to the neck of sick infants.

References

Appadurai, Arajun, and Carol Breckenridge. 1976. "The South Indian Temple Authority, Honor, and Redistribution". *Contributions to Indian Sociology. n.s.* 10.

Babb, L.A.1975.*The Divine Hierarchy, Popular Hinduism in Central India.* New York: Columbia University Press.

Bagchi, P. C .1998, 1983. "Some Linguistic Notes," In N. NathLaw (ed.), The Indian Historical Quarterly 1925, 1963, Vol.IX, article 63. Delhi, Caxton.

Bhattacharyya, N.N. 1977. The Indian Mother Goddess. New Delhi: Manohar Publishers.

Clothey, F.W.1978. "*The Many Faces of Murukan: The History and Meaning of a South Indian God*". Mouton: The Hague.

Capalan. 1987. *Class and Culture in Urban India. Fundamental in a Christian Community.* Oxford: Oxford University Press.

Dumont, Louis.1986. *A South Indian Subcaste: Social Organisation and Religion of the Pramalai Kallars*. Delhi: Oxford University Press.

Fuller, Christopher, J.1992. "*The Camphor Flame: Popular Hinduism and Society in India*". Princeton: N.J. Princeton University Press.

Hassan, K.A.1967.*The Cultural Frontier of Health in Village India*. Bombay: Manaktala and Sons Pvt. Ltd.

Inden, Ronald, B.1976. *Marriage and Rank in Bengali Culture*. Berkeley: University of California Press. Institution of Hinduism.

Jacob, Pandian, E.T.1975. "Nadu Veedu Rituals and Family Shamanism in Tamil Society: A Cult Institution of Hinduism". *Man in India*.55 (1).

Jagadisa Ayyar, P.V. 1992. *South Indian Customs*. New Delhi: Asian Educational Services.

Kjaerholm, Lars. 1984. Aiyanar and Aiyappan in Tamil Nadu : Change and Continuity in South Indian Hinduism. *Folk*. 26 (Copenhagen).

Moffat, Michael. 1976. *An Untouchable Community in South India: Structure and Concensus*. Princeton: Princeton University Press.241

Nishimura, Yuko. 1987. *A Study of Maariyamman Worship in South India: A Preliminary study on Modern South Indian Villages Hinduism*. Tokyo: ILCAA.

Nobokov, Isabelle.1995. "*Who are You?" Spirit Discourse in a Tamil World*. Ph.D. Dissertation. Berkeley: University of California Press.

Ostor, Akos.1980.*The Play of the Gods: Locality, Ideology, Structure, and Time in the Festivals of a Bengali Town*. Chicago: University of Chicago Press.

Petitet, H.P. and Pragathi, V. 2007. Ethnographic views on the *Valaikaappu*: A Pregnancy rite in Tamil Nadu. *Indian Anthropologist*. Vol. 37. No. 1. Jan-June 2007.

Raheja, Gloria, Goodwin, J.1988. *The Position in the Gift: Ritual, Presentation and the Dominant Caste in the North India Village*. Chicago: The University of Chicago Press.

Rao, Sudhakar. 1991. "Religion of Endavur Untouchables". *The Eastern Anthropologist*. Vol. 44, 2.

Srinivas, M.N. 1965. *Religion and Society Among the Coorgs of South India*. Bombay: Asia Publishing House.

Thurston, E.B. 1975 (1909). *Castes and Tribes of Southern India.* Vol. 5.Madras Government Press.

Turner, Victor. 1967. *The Forest Symbols.* Ithaca. N.Y.: Cornell University Press.

Wadley, Susan Snow.1975. *Shakti: Power in the Conceptual Structure of Karimpur Religion*. Chicago: The University of Chicago Press.

Whitehead, Henry.1921. *The Village Gods of South India.* Second Edition. Calcutta: Association Press and London: Oxford University Press.

18

The Study of Nayar Lineage

— *Varun Thampan*

Introduction

According to the definition of Notes and Queries, "A lineage consists of all the descendants in one line of a particular person through a determinate number of generations. ......, a matrilineage consists of all the descendants through females of a single ancestress. Where the living members of a lineage form a recognized social group it may be called a lineage group". A large lineage group, i.e., one whose members are being separated by several generations from the founding ancestor, may be divided into segments or sub-lineages, each consisting of the descendants of some descendant of the founder of the whole lineage.....In most societies, the lineage is exogamous...A lineage may be identified by exclusive ritual observances of a totemic or other kind, may have common or joint property rights over land, watering places or herds." (1951)

Kinship and lineage are indispensable elements of a social structure. "Kinship is relationship actually or putatively traced through parent-child or sibling relations, and recognized for social purposes....Matrilineal or uterine kinship is kinship traced through females only....Kinship system...denote the pattern of social usages observed in the reciprocal behavior of persons who are, or are regarded as being related by kinship or affinity." (Notes and Queries, 1951). "Ritual, like etiquette, is a formal mode of behavior recognised as correct......it implies the belief in the operation of supernatural agencies or forces. Religion is characterised by a belief in, and an emotional attitude towards, the supernatural being or beings, and a formal mode of approach – ritual – towards them. There are usually myths connected with the body of beliefs, and these are reflected in both form and content of the ritual." (Notes and Queries, 1951). This paper explains the relevance of kinship and ritual in the context of a Nair matrilineage in north Malabar region.

Historical Sketch

Nayar is a caste local to Kerala State in southern India. They rank high in caste hierarchy. Their traditional role was that of soldier nobility. They follow matrilineal pattern of inheritance. Their lineages were called *Taravad*, which finds split into large number of *Taivazhi* or sub-lineages. Usually, the members of same lineage or sub-lineage lived in the same household[1]. Each lineage was based around a manorial estate and had the tutelary goddess of its own. Each lineage was a property owning corporate body, which was also a part of feudal military network. The eldest men of lineage were members of Nayar caste guild, which commanded considerable political power in the medieval Kerala (Logan, 1887). Men of each lineage had to join armies in the time of war. In central and southern Kerala, the pattern of residence after marriage was to hang on local customs with growing children in their Taravad manor. In the pre-modern era, they practiced polyandry. In the case of northern Kerala, the pattern of such residence after marriage was virilocal with women returning to Taravad manor only, in case of her widowhood or divorce. Until early 20th century, they practiced hypergamy with superior ranking Namboothiri Brahmins and Malayali Kshatriyas. (Gough, 1961) (Fuller, 1974).

Geographic boundary of northern Kerala is Korapuzha River[2] in south and Chandragiri River[3] in north. It is bound in the west by Arabian Sea and in the east by Mysore Plateau. Right up to early 20th century, a taboo forbade the marriage between Nayar woman of northern Kerala and Nayar man from central/southern Kerala and also forbade the travel of Nayar women outside northern Kerala. (Panikkar, 1900) (Fawcett, 1901) (Thurston, 1909) The Origin of this custom is not known, though it had become weak due to passage of time. Area of study for this paper is Kurumathur, which lay east of Thaliparamba, Cannanore district. Lineage studied is named *Puthenveedu*[4]. They belong to Nambiar sub-caste within larger Nayar community. This area is being located four kilometres north of the state highway that runs from Thaliparamba to Sreekandapuram.

This lineage, as per admission of its members, is of entirely local origin without connecting any distant area. This lineage has many cadet lineages that are spread across the larger area in this (Thaliparamba) taluk. The sub-lineage chosen for this paper alone had some seventy two members. This lineage has fraternal ties with other two lineages. One of them is being located in close proximity, whereas the other is based in the coastal area, twenty km to west. Members of these three lineages treat one another as part of one single larger lineage and so sexual or marital relation between them were being forbidden. Also, they share the same tutelary deity.

In the early 20th century, this lineage was one of the many well-to-do commoner lineages. But, it was not always so. They claim selves to be of aristocracy, which fell in the rank during hard times. Men of this lineage acted as commandants over a part of Kuppam[5] valley for Chirakkal[6] Raja. During the invasion of Tipu Sultan, their wealth and many of the men were perished in war. They were reduced to penury by the time Sultan's troops left the area. But, a woman of this lineage stumbled upon a treasure so they could revive their lost fortune. But, the annexation of princely state of Chirakkal by the British in the early 19th century meant that they lost their political importance and military role.

Once they lost the military and political roles, they concentrated entirely on agriculture. They had a large manor and possessed nearly twelve square km of land. Their landed estates covered fields, fallows, meadows and forests. Until early 20th century, this continued to be the case. After that, mismanagement and property dispute led to the destruction of collectively held property of lineages. These issues have ensured death to joint family system as members started to set up separate nuclear households. Manor house was also demolished in the end and by 1980; the lineage was not in possession of single cent of land as the collective property.

Religious Lore – A Look

Like most Nayar lineages, this lineage too had *Shakti* as tutelary deity. They call her *Paraliamma*. She is associated with Mookambika Devi. It is believed that once a *Karanavar*[7] of this lineage, who was a great devotee of Mookambika Devi, went on a pilgrimage to Kollur. The Goddess, who was pleased with his devotion accompanied him back home. When *Karanavar* saw to his amazement that Goddess had accompanied him, he installed her in the *Kottilakam*[8] of manor house. Since that day, the members of this lineage venerate this man as their *Guru*. A custom was that worship of *Paraliamma* should be done only after veneration of *Guru*.

Along with *Paraliamma*, the sub-deities were also venerated. It is believed that the sub-deities acted as retainers of *Paraliamma*. They are *Kummiamma*, *Adala*

Bhagavati and *Vannathi Pothi. Kummiamma* acted as companion of *Paraliamma. Adala Bhagavati* is the bodyguard of *Paraliamma. Vannathi Pothi* is the washerwoman of *Paraliamma. Paraliamma, Kummiamma* and *Adala Bhagavati* are worshipped in the form of swords on wooden platforms. *Vannathi Pothi* has only a wooden platform and no sword. *Kottilakam* where four deities were installed remained shut throughout the year. Only on two days a year will the *Kottilakam* be opened. But kinsmen are free to pray from outside. On either side of the door of *Kottilakam* have lamps fixed to wall. These lamps are lit daily at twilight by members of lineage. Close to *Kottilakam, Guru* also has a room allotted for him - *Gurusthanam.* In this room, a lamp is put on a wooden platform to symbolize the *Guru. Gurusthanam* remains closed for whole years save the two special days. Door of this room too has lamps flanked on left and right. Lamps are lit here too on twilights of each day.

A development has occurred eighteen years ago. During an astrological consultation, it was discovered that there was presence of *Kuttichchatan*[9] (also known as *Shasthappan)* in the vicinity of *Kottilakam and it* was decided that a spot should be allotted for *Kuttichchatan* also. So, a stone platform was built for *Kuttichchatan* west to the seat of *Guru* at a distance of five metre. *Theyyam*[10] was also conducted for *Kuttichchatan* along with the rest of deities. But soon, the members of the lineage ended the conduct of *Theyyam* for *Kuttichchatan.* Instead a *Puja* by Namboothiri Brahmins was being conducted. Today, a lamp is being lighted each day at the twilight on the stone platform for *Kuttichchatan.*

Sacred performances are being conducted only on three days in the whole year. Only on these days are Kottilakam and room of Guru opened for worship. When the Moon moves into asterism of Krittika with the siderial Sun in Scorpio (*Vrischikatile Karthika*), Namboothiri Brahmins hold *Ganapati Puja* followed by *Paraliamma.* It is being believed that this day is being the birthday of *Paraliamma.* This day usually falls between November 15 and December 16.

Second day comes, when the siderial Sun hits 16th degree in Aquarius (*Kumbham Patinaaru*). It happens between February 15 and March 15. It is on this day that *Theyyam* is being conducted in the honour of *Paraliamma* and her aides. Firstly, Namboothiri Brahmins conduct *Ganapati Puja* followed by the *Puja* for *Kuttichchatan.* In the twilight hours, the performance of *Theyyam* commences. *Theyyam* is being conducted from two specialists of Velan caste. First, *Theyyam* to be performed is for *Vannathi Pothi* by one of the specialist. Then, the second specialist performs *Theyyam* for *Adala Bhagavati* followed by Theyyam for *Kummiamma Theyyam* and finally *Theyyam* for *Paraliamma.* A member of the lineage acts a *Komaram.* He assists *in the Theyyam* during the overall performance.

By dawn, all the four *Theyyam* performances will be over. The devotees come to seek primarilyt the blessings of *Paraliamma..* They hail from a wide range of spectrum – members of the lineage, offspring of male members of that lineage, affinal kin of the members of lineage, locals who come from a variety of castes and on the occasion, even persons from distant areas come to seek blessings sharing with grievances and seeking answers to riddles and questions. *Theyyam* blesses them and give answers to their riddles. They make offerings of money to him. The members of the lineage often undertake promise (*Prarthana Parayal*) to *Paraliamma.* Often, they pledge to conduct *Theyyam* of a year or make similr pledge to conduct a *Kolathumakolam.* The latter is a practice, where the *Theyyam* performance is repeated after the usual performance. This performance is conducted only on special request by parties who had done *Prarthana Parayal.*

Paraliamma is associated with fertility. The devotees of *Paraliamma* believe that one of the consequences of her wrath would be childlessness. Her blessings give the person concerned with healthier and righteous children.

On the third day after *Theyyam*, the ceremony of *Kariyadi* is conducted. On this day, *Kottilakam* finds opened. After its performance, the entire sacred site finds left as it was. No cleaning will follow. On the day of *Kariyadi*, Namboothiri Brahmins were being employed. First, a *Ganapati Puja* with that dedicated to *Paraliamma* will be on. The entire sacred site finds thoroughly cleaned

Area where this sacred site found located is known as *Kottam*. The rectangular plot lay facing east. On the left side of *Kottilakam* is *Gurusthanam*. *Kuttichchatan* occupy in its front. A wall surrounds the entire plot and towards the north is a well and rectangular shaped house. Nobody lives in that house. But, bronze lamps and wares needed for sacred ceremonies were stored. The entire *Kottam* finds covered by GI sheets mounted on four huge metallic pillars. A small wicket gate will be on the west of the plot.

This lineage has a tradition of white magic. Some of its members were well known magicians in the past centuries. But that tradition has died out completely like their warrior past. The decline and destruction of that lineage as a traditional property owning corporate body had its impact on the religious practice. As reckless *Karanavars* alienated the entire property, even the area of what is being now *Kottam*[11] found lost to the lineage. It ended up with the son of a *Karanavar*. Originally, the manor house of the lineage stood on what is now *Kottam*. *Kottilakam* of *Paraliamma* was demolished during the demolition of manor house, The performance of ceremonies ceased in this spot (even though some devout members of the lineage continued the conduct of religious ceremonies at their houses. This situation lasted for some thirty years). In the past, it was said that *Shakteya Puja*[12] or the worship using *tantric* rites was conducted. Similarly, the sacrifice of fowl was originally practiced, but no longer practiced today, as it was decided that butchery in the name of religion is not required. Another ritual that previously conducted, but now abandoned was *Pattam Udayam.* This was conducted when the sidereal Sun entered 10th degree in Libra sign.

The passage of time has destroyed most aspects of traditional life of this Nayar lineage. Manor house, collective property, joint family, martial training, white magic and *tantric* rites erre only distant memory. But basic element of religious life remained in tact. It was due to this fact that many members of this lineage continued to perform sacred ceremonies associated with the lineage deities even after the alienation of traditional sacred spot. Many members of the lineage became concerned when the bevy of astrologers predicted tutelary deity as angry with the members of lineage. It was concluded that in order to propitiate the lineage deity, alienated *Kottam* area must be recovered, sacred building must be rebuilt and the ceremonies be restored. One wealthy member of the lineage remedial actions single-handedly. He was later joined by other members of his lineage. Today, the cost of rituals and ceremonies in *Kottam* finds shared or sponsored by the members.

Conclusion

The religious life of the Nayar lineage described above evinced that right from the inception; it showed unmistakable intrinsic features in the Little Tradition as well as special characteristics belonging to the Great Tradition. The conduct of *Theyyam* belongs to the Little Tradition, whereas the ceremonies that employ Brahmin priests fall with the Great Tradition. The concepts of Universalisation and Parochialisation can also be witnessed in this case. *Paraliamma* is the parochialised form of *Mookambika Devi*; whereas the Universalisation was found in action through the linking of *Kuttichchatan* to Lord *Vishnu.*

It must be noted that the members of this lineage in contrast with their ancestors have become much more involved in the great traditions of Hinduism. They visit Hindu holy areas like Guruvayur, Sabarimala, Kollur and Palani. Many have become better versed in the philosophical aspects of great Hindu traditions like Epics and Puranas. But in spite of that, their faith in traditional religious practices with temporary eclipse - have made them align intact. The point to be noted here is that matrilineage remained intact as a unit of kinship to this day despite the total destruction of lineage as the corporate entity with political, economic and military role and as a property owning body. The survival of matrilineal kinship ensured that built-in kinship has also survived. It was only because of this reason that a revival of the traditional sacred practice was feasible.

Bibliography

Fawcett, F. 1985 (1901), *Nayars in Malabar,* New Delhi: Asian Educational Services.

Fuller, C.J. 1976, *Nayars Today,* London: Cambridge University Press.

Gough, Kathleen and David Schneider eds. 1961, *Matrilineal Kinship,* Berkeley and Los Angeles: University of California Press.

Committee of Royal Anthropological Institute of Great Britain and Ireland. (1951). *Notes and Queries of Anthropology.* London: Routledge and Kegan Paul Ltd.

Logan, William. 2012 (1887). Malabar Manual, New Delhi: Asian Educational Services.

Panikkar, T.K. Gopal.1983 (1900), *Malabar and Its Folk,* New Delhi: Asian Educational Services.

Thurston, Edgar. 1987 (1909), *Castes and Tribes of South India,* Vol. 5, New Delhi: Asian Educational Services.

Notes

1. If population of a lineage is too big, a part of it either may live in separate house or form a sub-lineage.
2. This river is only a few miles north of Calicut town.
3. River lay immediate south of Kasargode town.
4. Name of lineage is imaginary. This is done to protect identity.
5. This river lay north of Thaliparamba town.
6. A princely state which covered much of Cannanore district
7. Eldest male in a Nayar lineage is called Karanavar. He also acts as the supreme head of the lineage.
8. Room that lay to the left of inner verandah.
9. He is considered an element of Lord Vishnu.
10. This is a ritual dance that is part of popular Hinduism in Northern Kerala.
11. It lay with face towards east. It is a rectangular plot. On the left side of *Kottilakam* is *Gurusthanam*. In front of *Gurusthanam* is the seat of *Kuttichchatan*. A wall surrounds the entire plot and towards the north is a well and rectangular shaped house.
12. Local expression for the worship of Shakti through *tantric* rituals.

Index

C

L

M

N

O

P